1966
UNCOVERED

1966
UNCOVERED

The Unseen Story of the World Cup in England

Peter Robinson and Doug Cheeseman
Text by Harry Pearson

MITCHELL BEAZLEY

1966 UNCOVERED
Produced by Peter Robinson and Doug Cheeseman
Text by Harry Pearson
Edited by Philip Cornwall

First published in Great Britain in 2006 by Mitchell Beazley,
an imprint of Octopus Publishing Group Ltd,
2–4 Heron Quays, London E14 4JP

ISBN 13: 9 78184533 235 8
ISBN 10: 1 84533 235 0

A CIP catalogue record for this book is available from the British Library

Set in Scala Sans LF

Printed and bound in China

Commissioning Editor Jon Asbury
Senior Editor Peter Taylor
Production Gary Hayes
Proofreader Richard Guy
Indexer Sue Farr

Previous page **Alf Ramsey assesses the
task in hand in his office in early 1966**
Monte Fresco, Mirror

Right **Anticipating busy roads near
Wembley. Some of the 1400 direction signs
the AA erected await distribution**
Peter Skingley, United Pictures International

1966
CONTENTS

Bobby Charlton,
Old Trafford,
Manchester 2005
Peter Robinson

1966 FOREWORD

Bobby Charlton & Franz Beckenbauer

In conversation with Peter Robinson, former Fifa official photographer

Bobby Charlton was born in 1937. The 1966 World Cup finals were his third; the first, in Sweden in 1958, came a few months after he survived the Munich air crash. His last England match, his 106th, was the 3-2 World Cup quarter-final defeat against West Germany in 1970.

***Peter Robinson* You come from the north-east, an area known for hard graft. What did you bring into football from your background as a miner's son?**
Bobby Charlton The work ethic – my dad never shirked a day's work in his life and always said you didn't get anything unless you really battled for it. My football life has been a sweat: every moment you change into the gear you're expected to sweat and at the end of any match if you've done your job properly you've got to be tired.

I remember just before the 1966 semi against Portugal one of the papers, it might have been the *Daily Sketch*, offered to bring my mam and dad down to London for the game. But my dad said he couldn't come because he was working. Just think: that's the semi-final of the World Cup and he couldn't come because he was working and it would mean him missing his shift at the pit.

You had played for England since 1958. How quickly did things change when Alf Ramsey took over?
After four months, I thought something different was happening. I could really sense what the team was going to become. Even before then, most of the players who were involved in the World Cup in Chile, under Walter Winterbottom, thought we had a great chance at home in '66 because the players were good enough and all we really had to do was to play to our best.

Before Ramsey came along you were supposed to look like an England player and if you didn't you never got picked, but Alf wasn't bothered about any of that – he would pick people like Nobby Stiles and my brother Jack, who were not what you would call classical players in any form but nobody could do the job better than them.

Take Nobby. What did you want from him? To win the ball. You didn't expect him to be charging up the field, doing one-twos. He had an ability to sniff danger, and you can't teach people this.

I would say you could call him a great player. That's what Alf Ramsey could see in the players he picked, that's what he brought to the job. He did the lot.
How did the build-up to '66 go?
Before we got anywhere near the finals, Alf tried everybody, tried different systems, tried different pairings. But he knew what he was looking for and knew when he needed to have it ready. And he took us on really hard trips abroad, we played every hard team there was to play and the outcome was that by '66 we weren't afraid of anybody. In that period up to the finals we lost only once in two years.

We had a system that worked. Team talks were brief and to the point because we were winning. I don't think he doubted for a moment that we were going to win the cup.
One criticism levelled in some newspapers was that 1966 was "the World Cup of fouls". Is that fair?
The only match that might produce that quote would be Brazil v Portugal. The Portuguese did kick people unashamedly, possibly because they thought there was no way they were going to win against Brazil without being brutal.
Your quarter-final against Argentina didn't fit into that category, then.
No. Argentina were what you expect: they didn't come to kick us, they came to stop us from playing. They were dangerous, they were big tough lads, skilful and uncompromising, but not kickers.
What do you remember about your opening game, the goalless draw against Uruguay?
It was difficult. We knew about South American defences. They, too, were uncompromising, using tricks that were not what we thought of as part of our game, such as holding on to people's shirts.

But despite knowing that, maybe it was first-game nerves or the country's expectations that produced the result.
You scored England's first goal, against Mexico in the second game, after a run from the centre circle. As well as it being a great shot, did you feel your goal helped the country relax, particularly after the tension of that 0-0 draw with Uruguay?
Yes, I felt the goal was that important, too. To be honest I had had no intention of shooting, I was just taking the ball into their territory. If you run away quickly for the first 10 or 20 yards, once you

get the ball into defensive areas you stop people chasing you and that's what I did.

Roger Hunt had gone on this fantastic decoy run. I got within range and they were all looking at him. I always thought someone would come at me, but they didn't. I had always felt I could score goals from around about the box, particularly at Wembley because it was such a nice sweet surface. I just pinged it and... pewww... it was in.

Because of the win we went into the France game with a different attitude – and that was a comfortable victory.
But there was an unfortunate incident, with Nobby Stiles injuring Jacky Simon. The tackle was clearly not premeditated, but even you admit Stiles was a hard player. Franz Beckenbauer endorses that view, although he did say it with a laugh.
I can understand that and I think a lot of what Franz says, but Nobby disturbed people and frightened them and if you're a defender that's what you ought to aim for. But because he was a little abrasive, it always had an effect on the other team. Anyone that criticized Nobby probably respected him, too, and it usually meant they didn't want to play against him. That was probably what Beckenbauer meant.
This is a book about photographs and photographers, as well as the World Cup. Leaving the football for a moment, what was or even is now your view on photographers and photography?
I'm generally impatient with photographers. I can't understand why they take 40 or 50 pictures and might not even put one of them in the paper and why they always seem to ask for a bit more than they actually deserve. But they always seemed to get us to do what they wanted. I still get impatient when they say "Can you just do one more?" or "Can you do this pose?" or "Can you stand on your head?" or whatever. I usually think there's no point in arguing with them, I simply suffer them.
As a photographer myself I'm sorry to hear that... but can you remember anyone in particular that wasn't quite that bad?
Yes, there was a local lad here called Roy Broom – he lived quite close to me and was a member of the golf club near where I lived. And there was Ray Green, of course. He worked for one of the "good" papers. He took a really good picture of me in

Bobby Charlton & Franz Beckenbauer

action, down on my knee. It won some award – football picture of the year or whatever. I have a copy of that one.

Returning to the World Cup, what was your preparation and the mood in the country like in the days leading up to the final?

This may seem strange, but we weren't really aware of the mood in the country other than what we saw in the papers, because we were shepherded away from it all. We weren't even allowed to see our wives till near the semi-final, when they were invited to Hendon for a meal then went away again.

On that morning of the final, me and Ray Wilson – who always shared the same room – went out to Golders Green high street to do some shopping. There was a dinner that night, win or lose, and we were due to see our wives for the first time in a while. So we thought we should go out and buy a new shirt. And really there was no fuss at all, no one bothered and we were left to shop in peace.

The only thing I remember of anything close to a reaction in the streets was the day of the semi-final, going from our Hendon hotel to Wembley – the fire station had the fire brigade ringing the bell because they knew we always passed there on the way to the ground. But after that it was pretty much plain driving, with nothing in the streets. It wasn't the sort of area with a lot of housing close up.

What were the tactics for the final?

For the first 15 minutes I think most players were trying to work out what they were supposed to be doing, but my role was clear in my mind as I was concentrating on Beckenbauer: my instructions were that this was how we were going to win.

What was behind this decision?

Alf told us that the only person who could do us any damage was Beckenbauer, because he was young and impetuous and didn't always do what people told him to. When he got the ball he went into positions in the box that would be really dangerous.

So in the few minutes before getting ready to go out, Alf took me aside and said: "I want you to stick with Beckenbauer, you've got a good engine and if you can stick with him we can win." Of course I was disappointed. Here I was in the World Cup final and someone tells you to mark a man and I had never been asked to man-mark in my life, never ever.

Almost from the whistle we were with each other. I was watching him and he was watching me. And years later I found out that Helmut Schön, the West Germany manager, told him the same thing and had given him the same instruction about me.

Both Schön and Beckenbauer were apparently heavily criticized afterwards for this because Beckenbauer never went forward into the box as he had done in all their previous games.

So the two of us never took part in the game, but it was a crucial decision by Alf because Beckenbauer was their most dangerous player. If for a moment I had felt a little bit selfish and decided to go up, thinking "maybe I'll find something", and there had then been a breakaway and suddenly he'd been 40 or 50 yards away, it would have been the difference between winning and losing. The concentration was intense and it was exhausting – we both ran a lot without the ball. But we had to... quite a joke really.

That's why I found it impossible to find a picture from the final of you or Beckenbauer without the other being in the shot. What do you remember of how the game went, starting with their early goal?

Ray Wilson made the mistake. He headed the ball back and Helmut Haller picked it up and it just crept in past Gordon Banks. I thought: "Bloody hell, that's not like him. But heck, it's early enough, still time." And then Bobby Moore got a free-kick and took it quickly – which was unusual, normally you give people the chance to consolidate their positions – and it dropped for Geoff Hurst completely on his own to head in, completely unmarked. I thought: "He's offside, he's got so much space. But no... a goal, that'll do me."

In the second half we were attacking on a regular basis, winning corners and free-kicks. Then Geoff Hurst hit the ball back into the area, it hit the foot of a defender and it created a sort of top spin. It dropped right in front of Martin Peters, who didn't have to do anything except let it hit his foot.

I thought we could hang on, but you've got to remember everyone was knackered. It had been a hard season, 11 months solid football for us, then the World Cup. It was a slog out there, but we thought we could hold out.

We didn't do anything wrong, apart from a debatable free-kick the referee gave against my

brother, our Jack. The ball bounced in the box and whatever bit of luck there was going it seemed that they got it. A shot was blocked and it moved across, then suddenly it just dropped right for the player. He hadn't worked himself into the position, he just happened to be there and side-footed it in.

We were ready for extra time, we had trained for it and we were fit, but what I remember most was that all we were concerned about was whether the break might have affected our concentration. At the first break Alf told us to stand up and not to sit down because if we showed that we weren't tired it might reflect on how they were feeling. And we stood up and we went out and got the third goal.

I guess it's inescapable that we have to talk about whether the ball crossed the line.

It's been done to death. Whenever any of the Germans ask me about it, I always say: "Are you suggesting that if that goal hadn't happened you would have beaten us?" Not one of them says yes, they would, because there was no way they were going to beat us.

What was Ramsey's response once you had won? From the photographs we've seen, the only way I can describe it is "shell-shocked".

Well he had done what he was good at, all the planning and preparation, but he wasn't ready for the winning bit. He wasn't clear what to expect or how to react, particularly on the field. Possibly he was keeping his emotions under control. But he warmed later to the idea. At the Royal Garden Hotel he was a bit well oiled, so he was all right.

The players' celebrations at the end are legendary – it was very emotional.

When the final whistle went I blubbed. I'm not embarrassed to say that was so. Maybe I had been hugging Nobby because Nobby was around me always, and my brother came across and our Jack says: "What about that, what about that then." I said: "I don't think our lives will ever be the same again." And that's exactly the way of it. There hasn't been one day since that someone hasn't mentioned it, not one day in my whole life.

Can you recall the scenes in the streets on the way from Hendon to the celebration dinner at the Royal Garden Hotel in Kensington High Street?

Beckenbauer and Charlton, stride for stride during the final
Sven Simon

Yes. This was the first time, after being more or less locked away for three weeks, when I really felt we got the mood of the country. We drove through north London, Notting Hill and Bayswater and there wasn't a window that didn't have someone in it. As we went along I thought about what would have happened if we had lost. I had never even given it a thought. What about all these people that are hanging out the windows now and are so happy? I said to Ray Wilson: "What would we have done if we had lost?"

Playing for your club and your country is different – with your club it's with your working lads. But playing for your national team you're responsible for your whole country. There's 11 of you and you're playing against another 11 to become the best 11 on the planet.

It's something very different from the European Cup or whatever, that can't be anywhere like the same as the World Cup.

With Manchester United and all the things that have happened to this club, of course, it's marvellous, but it's still only a personal thing. But for the national team it's not personal, it's more, it's a duty, and if you play for England then something special is expected.

One final thought on the game. It was played, I believe, without any cynicism, pettiness or rancour – a great advert for sportsmanship. But how do you see it now in its simplest sense, as a game, a game of football?

It was a great final. Everybody wants goals, everybody wants drama, good saves, controversy, and it was packed with them. But it was intense. In extra time I never looked at how long there was to go because if I thought there was two minutes to go it may have been really six or seven minutes. I was afraid to look because I was so tired.

When Bobby Moore picked the ball up at the end and then carried it out of trouble, everybody was panicking and saying kick the bloody thing. He didn't, and brought it back on to his right foot and saw Geoff Hurst and let him have it. By then their defence were shattered – they were nowhere near him and he went on and finished it off...

It was great!

It was, and thank you.

Franz Beckenbauer was born in 1945. He was playing in his first World Cup. He lost a final in 1966 and a semi-final in 1970, before lifting the trophy as captain at home in 1974. He managed West Germany to the 1986 final and their 1990 win.

Peter Robinson What were you like when you were growing up in Munich?
Franz Beckenbauer I had one interest only: I was football mad. We lived in the district of Giesing and every hour I could find I played football in the street – kicking the ball against the wall learning how to control it, nothing tactical just play. Later I wasn't interested in the usual 1960s things – politics, the student movements of the time and so on. I was always football, football, football.

But when you left school you had a proper job.
I joined an insurance company, Allianz, when I was 14 and stayed for three or four years, until Bayern offered me a contract, around 1962-63. Now Allianz is probably Europe's biggest insurance company. Even Munich's new stadium is the Allianz Arena.

It's hard to imagine Franz Beckenbauer selling insurance.
For me too, now.

Bayern weren't in the *Bundesliga* when you signed. When did you make your top-flight debut?
That was on 14 August 1965.

Less than a year later you're in a World Cup final – quite some progress.
Well, it's not as impressive as it sounds: we simply won promotion to the *Bundesliga*.

Just over a month after that first top-flight game and 15 days after your 20th birthday, you made your Germany debut on 26 September, in a qualifier against Sweden in Stockholm which you won. How did you prepare for the finals?
As well as friendlies, we went to Malente, a health spa in the north. In 1990, when I coached the team, I took them there for a week, partly because of history but really because of superstition.

I know you're big on superstition – I photographed you throughout that 1990 World Cup and you insisted on wearing the same jacket, shirt and tie at every game. It seemed to work, because you won.
We had two afternoon games and it was really hot, but I still wore the jacket. The sweat was running

like water into my shoes – well, that's superstition.
Was the 1966 World Cup your first visit to England?
We had a friendly in February that year; Nobby Stiles scored, something he almost never did.
When you arrived for the tournament, what were your training sessions and press conferences like?
There were a lot of English fans and Germans, too, at training, but that's always been a tradition with the national team as long as I can remember. And the English were wonderful. I know your papers now go crazy about the war, but back in 1966 there was none of that and the public were wonderful.

What has changed today is the media situation. Now at a press conference there are 300 to 400 journalists, but in 1966 there were only five! And there was no television to speak of – the World Cup was on one channel only and if it was on back home it was just in black and white.

What about your contact with the press then – you spoke a little English?
No, nada – nothing. Bert Trautmann, who had played for Manchester City, was with us but as a trainer and adviser, not an interpreter.
What were the hotels and training facilities like?
The quality was very good. For us, England was the standard to aspire to, our dream, the motherland of football. Particularly for a young player like me, it was always a dream to play there. And it wasn't a disappointment. I especially remember the crowds, so many people and the atmosphere – super.
You were based in Derbyshire, in the Peak District – not quite Bavaria but beautiful nevertheless.
I remember, there was the hotel called "Peveril of the Peak". I remember this place after all this time – it was beautiful, but in the middle of nowhere, so you had a long trip in the bus to each game.

I particularly remember one trip to Birmingham. It took hours as usual and we had a stop, so someone arranged for us to go to the Dunlop tyre factory. Anyway, there was a long time before the game so they had found us a big room. There were not exactly beds, but mattresses on the floor and the whole team had a sleep. All 22 players in this big room in a factory for about one hour and then we get up and go to the stadium – that's how it was in 1966. I'll never forget this. It was probably Helmut Schön's idea.

Bobby Charlton & Franz Beckenbauer

What was your opinion of him? You were together through three World Cups, 1966, '70 and '74. Was he a good friend?

Yes, of course – he was fantastic, he was like a father. He was not a genius in tactics or training sessions, but he knew exactly what we liked to do to play. He gave us the ball and we just started to play – we played our own game. All the players liked coming to the national team for games, because the coach was Helmut Schön. Everybody liked him, everybody except the press, but that's not unusual.

What part did his assistants Dettmar Cramer and Udo Lattek play in all this?

Dettmar Cramer was responsible for the tactics, our Einstein, and Udo, who was very young, was just there for any help or support we needed.

The '66 tournament seems to have been a World Cup turning point for the German team – you have reached five finals since, while England have not been in any more.

The real start of this very successful time was getting the professional league – the *Bundesliga*. England had had a professional league since forever, but in Germany we had to wait until 1963.

Turning to the tournament, some in the press seemed to regard it as a rather violent World Cup.

Not by the standards of the time. Some games then were rough – against South Americans in particular – but not violent. We had only two rough games in 1966, against Argentina and Uruguay.

Why did Brazil, the holders, fail?

The kicking of Pelé was bad – he got badly hurt in the first game, kicked for half the game. But that wasn't the only reason – they were also in a very strong group, with Portugal and Hungary.

In the final, then, it must have been a relief to have two teams that wanted to play – no violence or, as you put it, "rough play".

No, I think there were too many elegant players, like Bobby Charlton. But if England needed the rough play you had Nobby Stiles, he was responsible for the rough play.

What was it like for you to come to London?

It was super to play at Wembley with 100,000 people, this was the Mecca of football. In Germany at this time we played in front of 15,000 maximum, now it was 100,000 – they made a big noise.

When you phoned home before the final, what was the feeling back in Germany?

No one expected us to get to the final, the whole country was dancing – just getting to the event was a success. We were complete underdogs, the outsiders, and qualification was really hard.

It was beautiful in the north, but we were glad to be in London. I think we went to some events that our embassy arranged for us, but I have forgotten now what they were.

When devising your tactics for the final, what did you know about England apart from what you learnt from the February friendly and those of their games that you were able to see on TV?

We were well briefed on all the players and operated a sort of man-marking system in our earlier games. So we did that totally for the final – Schnellinger against Ball, Weber against Hunt, Höttges played Hurst, Overath for Nobby. I played against Bobby Charlton – it was that simple, 10 pairs on the field.

So no more runs from midfield looking to score. How was that change put to you by Schön?

I knew about it some time before our usual tactics session, a day or more before the final. Schön wanted to get my reaction because this was different to the way I had been playing before. I said: "I will do whatever you want me to do, you're the boss. You give me the order and I will do what I have to do." It was a big job for me as a young player to play against the best man in the world, and Bobby Charlton was for me the best midfielder in the world. I didn't know, but years later Bobby told me exactly the same story – he had received the same order from Alf Ramsey to mark me... I was so surprised when he told me.

He was so strong – I was younger, but the game went into extra time and I must say I was so tired I really don't think I cared about winning or not. I was very, very happy once the game was finished.

Well the game may be finished but there's always *the* question – about whether Geoff Hurst's second goal, England's third, crossed the line. Your team-mate Wolfgang Weber's view is that "too much has been said about it, the goal stands, England were worthy champions". Uwe Seeler said: "The England team were exceptional, we accepted the outcome, we are good sportsmen." Sepp Maier, the reserve

goalkeeper, felt: "The linesman said the ball was in, that's that, I'm not bitter." Wolfgang Overath said: "England were a great side, we accepted defeat." I know you have been asked about this a 1000 times, but does Franz Beckenbauer say the same thing?

Of course, for sure. I don't know anything about the third goal – it was so quick I was only in the middle of the penalty area so I don't know whether it was in or out, behind the line, on the line or whatever.

There's all this business now about some technical device that might say one way or the other, but I don't follow it. We're still talking about it 40 years later – but if we take all that away, what about the reaction and the discussion that comes from a mistake? In football you need this too, it's a vital part of the game.

The enthusiasm and the reaction has to come from that argument, the debate. We need all this – imagine what you talk about in the office the next day if everything is decided eventually by some technical device. You know, whenever I come to England, the taxi driver reminds me as soon as I get in the cab. He says: "Hey, was it a goal or not?" It's great having all this passion.

We're telling the story of the 1966 World Cup through the photographs, and after 40 years in this game I can safely say your football life has been well documented in pictures. I imagine you still know or knew some of the photographers very well. Whom do you remember from around that time?

There was Metelmann and Kaiser, I think both from Hamburg, but there was a special one, Sven Simon. He was the son of Axel Springer the publisher and an excellent photographer. He took some nice pictures of me before the 1966 World Cup.

In one I am wearing a tuxedo and playing with the ball – just super. He also took some great pictures of me in a forest. He was the man I remember most from that time, though sadly he later killed himself.

What has your relationship with photographers been like generally?

I enjoy photographs and photographers – most are just doing a job, acting decently and not looking for "tricky" shots. I think I am more friends with them than with journalists.

A good way to end, I think – thank you.

**Franz Beckenbauer,
Frankfurt 2005**
Peter Robinson

1966
INTRODUCTION

In the 40 years since the 1966 World Cup, the aura of the tournament has grown far beyond what was the case at the time. Certain photographs, the colour image of Bobby Moore on the shoulders of his team-mates being the most notable, have become not just icons but almost the only ones that can seem to do justice to what the England team achieved.

In late 2004, while working on a regular feature on archival football photography for the magazine *When Saturday Comes*, the picture below, showing the scene of that famous shot of Moore, came up for inclusion. There must be 20-odd photographers gathered, so why is that one colour image so frequently used? Who were these photographers and what became of their work, not just that day but throughout the tournament? They must have produced a largely forgotten record of what remains a landmark in sport for countries as diverse as North Korea and Portugal. So the idea for *1966 Uncovered* began to take shape.

Working with Peter Robinson, the former official photographer for Fifa who had worked on World Cups from 1970 onwards, here was the chance to resurrect material, discovering the odd rarity that must be hidden away, and to deliver a fresh

perspective on a subject people think they know so well. To ensure that we produced a balanced record of the event and the 16 teams, we researched the material on the basis of the four regions that staged a group, with a special section for the final. All the pictures selected were taken in England and in 1966.

Then it got tricky. Ask Fifa, football's world governing body, about 1966 and they say it's the tournament from which they hold the least material – and this was the eighth World Cup. Ask David Barber, the FA's official historian, what the custodians of the English game possess and he'll explain that he inherited nothing from 1966. Derek Cattani, the FA's official photographer in 1966, lost the majority of his photos in a fire in 1970.

Furthermore most English papers have changed hands, sometimes without their archives (the Mirror Group own the 1966 pictures taken by the *Sun*, as Rupert Murdoch bought only the title when he acquired the paper in 1969), while of today's principal suppliers of sports photography, only the Press Association were operating at the time. Local papers, with honourable exceptions, often hold their archives in a disorderly state – if they have been kept at all.

What of the men behind the cameras? It was a prolific and imaginative age for British press photography, but the specialist sports photographer was in a distinct minority. Frank Baron, who later became one of the best known football men, was a darkroom boy at the Keystone agency and was amazed at how little interest regular news photographers had in football. They complained of long wet nights stuck at the wrong end to the action. With a thriving cultural, political and musical scene, the attraction of the game was not overwhelming. It was just another job, as some of the work logs that survive demonstrate. Agency and newspaper

staffers were as likely to get sent to an anti-Vietnam demonstration or the unveiling of a baby hippo at Coventry Zoo as a photoshoot with the Spain team. These same logs detail events involving such icons as the Beatles, Muhammad Ali and Frank Sinatra; you begin to realise (whisper it) that the World Cup in England was not a particularly big deal.

Accurately sourcing photos from 1966 was hampered by the photo pool system which meant material was distributed collectively by the agency pool BIPPA and the respective newspaper pools. Their roles are further explained in the Photography section on page 250. As a result, some valuable negatives were often anonymously sent round the press and chaotically handled. Thankfully, many of the BIPPA files remain intact at the Hulton Archive, now part of Getty Images, the Press Association collection has been opened up by the agency Empics and the *Mirror* have their negatives intact. But other collections have vanished and even establishing the original source of those surviving is difficult. To try to tell the story of the material itself, we have credited the original photographer or source in 1966, where possible, beneath the picture. The current distributors' details are on page 253.

We hope to have uncovered many photographs that have not been published since 1966 and in many cases not even then. Among the many unused negatives in the BIPPA brown envelopes was the shot of the North Koreans enjoying the clandestine western pleasures of a Laurel and Hardy film on page 22. The collection of the *Sunderland Echo* includes a trip to a local barbers by Soviet footballers in search of the *Man From U.N.C.L.E.* look seen on page 52. The *Birmingham Post* collection shows the city being spruced up: beige-coated men construct such municipal delights as the floral "living football" on page 68 and knock nails into visitor signs on page 82.

Merseyside gets into the World Cup spirit. Players from the four teams playing in the region go up in a window display in Claudia Street
Mercury Press

The material is also being uncovered in other ways. Many pictures were speedily printed or wired for newspaper use, then heavily cropped, often from large square negatives. This format was not ideal for the tight images favoured for news and sport, but lurking unwanted in the corners are the details that today help bring 1966 alive. On page 14, behind the unfazed Italy defender Roberto Rosato, a local casts a suspicious eye over the scene as a removals van goes about its business. The shot of Pelé jogging next to an eager fan on page 114 had been ignored, while a plain shot of him alone, tightly cropped, had been pulled out. As time has marched on the bespectacled autograph hunters, wonky helmeted police and incredulous passers-by have become a part of the story.

As well as a sense of football in its pre-commercial era, we hope to give you a flavour of England, a country still moving out of post-war austerity. See the unkempt state of the road outside Roker Park on page 39 and the residents of Liverpool painting their kerb stones on page 124 and decorating their windows (right) – images of hardy optimism reminiscent of the postwar *Picture Post*-era photography. England was still a firmly industrial country, too: look at Brazil training in Bolton, Spain at the Delta metalworks in Birmingham and North Korea at the ICI plant in Billingham. West Germany players, meanwhile, were handed a quaint rural billet in the Peak District. Many of the pictures chosen bring together the tournament with this sense of the time and place when they were taken.

For the famous picture of Moore, you will surely not have to look very far to find it in 2006. It will remain in demand and its aura will grow. No doubt too there is more photography still to be found, but in *1966 Uncovered* we hope to present a body of work that tells the full story of the time the World Cup came to England.

Doug Cheeseman

1966
NORTH EAST

The draw for the World Cup finals took place at the Royal Garden Hotel in Kensington, west London, on 6 January 1966. It was televised across western Europe and in all the participating nations with the obvious exception of North Korea. Of the 800 people there, 400 were reporters. As the official FA report would later observe in splendid Little Englander manner, "the babble of foreign tongues from the radio commentators in the gallery caused some inconvenience". Blathering continentals aside, the whole thing went off like clockwork.

Fifa had implemented a complicated series of seedings that effectively separated not only the two favourites, England and Brazil, from one another, but also ensured that the South American nations wouldn't meet one another at the group stage and the "Latin European countries" would likewise be kept apart. In such a way it was hoped to give each group a hint of mystery, a whiff of the exotic and "all-round spectator appeal". For Sunderland and Middlesbrough, hosts of Group Four, this meant Italy, Chile, the Soviet Union and North Korea. An interesting mixture culturally, for sure, but in football terms as likely to set the pulses racing as a mug of Horlicks and a pair of winceyette pyjamas.

This was a pity as in the north-east more than anywhere else the civic authorities were looking to the World Cup as a means of promoting the local area – of putting themselves "on the map". The region's only city, Newcastle, had not been selected as a venue. Middlesbrough and Sunderland were small, industrial towns. They were actually on the map, but in such fine print that they were easy to miss.

In Sunderland, the local liaison committee had been preparing for the influx of foreign fans since February 1965. They printed 21,450 copies of an information brochure on local amenities, 3,000 of which were sent to the Italian FA.

Nobody in Sunderland quite knew what to expect. The committee was not sure if it was "planning for 1000 or 10,000 visitors". In the end the numbers fell well short of that, with official visitor numbers put at 400 Italians, 200 Russians, 50 Chileans and no more than a dozen North Koreans. Bizarrely, despite the low turnout, accommodation still became a problem and when there was a sudden influx of British-based Italians the committee had to make an appeal on the BBC for people with spare rooms to come forward: 135 extra beds were found and a crisis averted.

A plan to use the mobile polling stations that toured mining villages at elections as visitor centres had to be abandoned: the police, who felt the World Cup wasn't quite as important as democracy, insisted the double-decker buses involved must be licensed and the cost was considered prohibitive. So three special centres were set up in temporary huts, local traders were chivvied to give their window displays "a festive air" and 300 sets of souvenir glasses engraved with "Sunderland scenes" were purchased as gifts for visiting teams and officials, though as it turned out only 201 of them were given away.

Interpreters staffed the visitor centres in Sunderland. On match days they were frequently called in by local shopkeepers to sort out problems. On one occasion a group of Italians grew agitated when their requests to see the Loch Ness monster were not met, while another party of four entered a restaurant and requested the owner give them use of the kitchen so they could cook their own dinner.

The official reception in Sunderland for the visiting squads on 14 July was a disappointing affair. Most of the players were not allowed to attend and, while 250 officials from the four teams did turn up, "language difficulties limited the circulation of the guests amongst the townspeople". The general air of anti-climax was also felt

at Seaburn Hall, where a special overseas visitors' club had been established. Sadly, the uptake of free membership was low. Local organizers reported that things might have been better had it not been for the chill of the Cold War, which meant that many Soviet visitors refused to fill in the membership forms "even though it was explained that this was merely a formality".

The authorities had actually gone out of their way to welcome the Soviets. In celebration of their visitors from beyond the Iron Curtain, the Empire Theatre in Sunderland engaged the services of the Georgian State Dance Company. The group proved hugely popular, drawing a total audience of 22,000 – more than watched some of the football matches.

Mind you, 5000 spectators also turned up to see a performance by 100 pipers and dancers from the north-east of England branch of the Scottish Pipe Band Association, so the local appetite for regimented folk activities was plainly keen.

Teesside, too, offered an Eisteddfod. For those whose taste didn't encompass dancers in national costume performing to traditional instruments, the Club Fiesta in Stockton-on-Tees promised international cabaret, which amounted to Tommy Cooper

After a two-day stay in Surrey, the Chile squad arrive at Newcastle station on 7 July
Sunderland Echo

and Bob Monkhouse, both of whom came from south of the Humber and therefore presumably qualified as continental. Military bands, greyhound racing, cricket, the occasional Gypsy ensemble and the odd open-air sculpture exhibition made up the rest of the entertainment.

The official overall guide for visitors to the tournament was remorselessly upbeat, sometimes optimistically so ("Manchester is in its own way as famous as Paris, New York or London"). "There is no shortage of entertainment of all types in Middlesbrough," it alleged, pointing out that this was the only large urban centre ever to make the final of Britain in Bloom.

The fact that games were being played there at all was a coup for Middlesbrough. Newcastle United, whose St James' Park was first choice, were locked in a bitter dispute with the council over their lease. The organizers sensed that this was not going to be resolved in time to carry out necessary remedial work, so St James' was dropped, providing welcome joy elsewhere. Boro had just been relegated to Division Three. Their Ayresome Park pitch was a byword for luxury, widely regarded as the best in England, but the ground itself was

in poor condition, however. Indeed, one Boro director, Charles Amer, viewed it as being in "a state of total disrepair". Luckily he owned a building firm that were happy to take on the task of bringing it up to scratch. Barriers on the terraces were strengthened, new seating was installed in several stands and hospitality facilities for visiting Fifa dignitaries were shoehorned into the area under the North Stand, despite some trouble with the sewers.

Harold Shepherdson was Boro's other contribution – the trainer had worked with the England side for some years. The chubby-cheeked, genial Shep had been with the squad in Chile at the 1962 finals, where one of his main tasks was forcing the players to take ping-pong ball-sized sulphur tablets to fend off stomach complaints.

The Italy players arrived at Teesside airport looking like they had just stepped off the set of Fellini's *La Dolce Vita*. Under their snappy suits they wore mid-blue shirts without – and this was enough to set jaws dropping – ties. The narrow, cobble-grey and brick-red streets of Sunderland and Middlesbrough seemed an unlikely backdrop for such exotica. To add to the incongruity, the Italians were billeted among the cattle, sheep and pigs of Durham Agricultural College. The World Cup was full of such weird juxtapositions. Uruguay were in Harlow, Mexico in Stamford Hill. Spain trained at the Delta Metals works ground in Erdington. Argentina had their first brush with the British police at their centre in Birmingham.

It is easy to see how the environment might have disorientated Italy. In the end, though, whatever it was that unsettled the handsome visitors seemed more internal than external. It shouldn't have been so, of course. Internazionale were one of Europe's top club sides, the Italian league the world's richest. Inter's Sandro Mazzola was a wiry, skilful striker with the pencil moustache of a gigolo; Gianni Rivera in

midfield had the unruffled air of an aristocrat; and defenders Tarcisio Burgnich and Giacinto Facchetti seemed to carry out their duties so effortlessly and impeccably it was a surprise to see mud on their knees.

Italy's first match was against Chile, who had qualified via a play-off victory over Ecuador. It was a rematch of the notorious 1962 Battle of Santiago. Anyone expecting a repeat of that game's unremitting violence was to be disappointed, however. Despite the history, the game, played in a steady drizzle, was totally devoid of both blood and thunder. Chile had one star, Luis Eyzaguirre, a full-back who was good enough to be selected for the Rest of the World side that played England at Wembley in 1963, to set against the glittering firmament that was the *Azzurri*. Italy emerged triumphant, winning 2-0 with goals from Mazzola and Paolo Barison, yet despite the presence of 5000 *tifosi* among the 27,000 in Roker Park they seemed uninspired, as if their thoughts were elsewhere, far from Seaburn and the north-east coast, in Portofino or Capri.

The North Korea team (or "the little men from the Land of the Morning Calm" as the correspondent of the *Times* dubbed them) had apparently lived for two years in a military barracks, training ceaselessly and, so rumour had it, celibately. Their coach Myung Rye-hyun was a full colonel in the People's Army and adopted commando-style methods. The last time a team from the peninsular had made the finals, South Korea in 1954, they had been let down by a lack of fitness. The North were determined that the same would not happen to them.

The North Korea team set out with the blessing of the Great Leader, Kim Il-sung, who advised them to embrace the energetic spirit of Chollima, the mythical winged horse of Korean legend and the name given to the Great Leader's post-war regeneration programme, of which the team were seen

as a symbol. More worryingly, the dictator also gave stern instructions that the players were not to lose all their matches. Given the nature of Kim Il-sung's regime it must have been clear to them that he would not react to defeat by simply throwing teacups.

The team were billeted in the comparative luxury of the St George Hotel (coincidentally owned by Boro director Charles Amer). They were a total mystery. They had qualified by beating Australia after every other Group 16 team – South Korea, Ghana, Guinea, Cameroon, Sudan, Algeria, Nigeria, Tunisia, Liberia, Senegal, Morocco, Mali, Ethiopia, Gabon, the United Arab Republic (Egypt) and Libya – withdrew in protest at the shortage of World Cup places available to African and Asian teams. Both games against Australia were played in the unlikely venue of Phnom Penh, Cambodia. A combined attendance of 88,000 saw the Koreans win 9-2 on aggregate. So far that was the sum total of their competitive matches. Nobody in England that summer, with the exception of Fifa president Sir Stanley Rous, had ever seen them play.

Some would have liked it kept that way. The Korean War had ended just 13 years before. The British Government didn't recognize North Korea. Nato had objected to their flag being flown. There was consternation over what might happen if North Korea's national anthem (*Aegukka*, or *Patriotic Song*, by Pak Se-yong: "The glory of a wise people/Brought up in a culture of brilliance" and so forth) got an airing, so Fifa decreed that the only time national anthems should be played before a match was for the opening game. In light of the international frostiness, the North Korea players were understandably nervous about the sort of reception they might get. "We thought of the English as the enemy," Pak Doo-ik recalled, "but they welcomed us."

That was particularly true of the supporters at Ayresome Park, who warmed to the North Koreans, cheering their every move in the opening match against the USSR. They were underdogs, played in red shirts like the town's side and trained at nearby Billingham Synthonia, so why not? The Soviets were a big bunch and towered

over the men from the Far East, none of whom was taller than 5ft 8in. North Korea's goalkeeper, Lee Chan-myung, was just 19, making him the youngest ever goalkeeper to appear in the finals, and the average age of the squad was just 22. It really did look like men against boys. Despite the Koreans' youthful zip, vigour and obvious fitness, the Soviets easily outplayed them, too, though such was the difference in size of the teams that it looked more like bullying. Eduard Malofeyev, twice, and Anatoly Banishevsky scored as they ran out 3-0 winners.

Only 13,792 turned up at Ayresome for the Koreans' next match, against Chile. The South Americans took the lead when Rubén Marcos converted a penalty after Oh Yoon-kyung had felled Pedro Araya, but in the second half the Koreans' fitness came to the fore and gradually they took control. In the game against the Soviet Union the pace of their play had been too frenetic, now they slowed it down slightly and started to pick out passes a bit better. In the 88th minute they grabbed an equalizer when Pak Seung-jin fired home a volley from the edge of the

Twenty-six single-decker Sunderland buses flew the flags of visiting teams alongside the Union Flag, in this case the Italian *tricolore* and the Soviet Union's hammer and sickle
Sunderland Echo

Blandford Street, Sunderland, modestly decked out for the tournament
Sunderland Echo

box. Afterwards a massive British sailor in full naval rig ran on to the field, hugged various Koreans and then paraded with them round the pitch. The Koreans wept, with a mixture of joy and relief – Kim Il-sung's instructions had been fulfilled.

The Soviet Union, referred to more or less universally as "the Russians", had a number of skilful individuals, including the winger Igor Chislenko, and defenders – organized by the mighty Albert Shesternev – who showed no compunction when it came to meting out punishment. In goal they had Lev Yashin, one of the game's superstars, a keeper who, it was claimed, combined the agility of a monkey with the elasticity of a squid and the manners of a gentleman. Yashin had saved more than 100 penalties. He dressed all in black and wore a flat cap; with his slim physique, feline grace and poise, the get-up suggested a flamenco dancer from Bolton. The Soviets called him "the Black Octopus".

The USSR were regarded as dour, obdurate and – surely the most popular adjective for teams from eastern Europe – well drilled, the sporting equivalent of the Red Army. Unsurprisingly, perhaps, given their dull, utilitarian reputation, they were lodging at Grey College in Durham.

As if to show their lighter side, one day when half the team were off taking a Turkish bath the rest invited two passing teenage postmen to join them in a kick-about. How involved Greg Walsh and Stuart Fitzgerald actually became may be gauged by the fact that one didn't bother taking off his jacket.

When the Soviet Union met Italy it was plain that a draw would suit both teams. Despite being handicapped by a strangely lopsided team and missing Rivera and Barison, Italy looked like a side capable of achieving a draw whenever they desired one, which was most of the time. Certainly the game lived down to the increasing conviction in the north-east that, as Michael Williams of the *Sunday Telegraph* reported, "you can see better games at Hartlepool in January".

Uninspiring and expressionless was the overriding impression of a match in which the only real dash of colour was created by the decision by Yashin to wear red gloves. Mazzola missed an early chance when through one-on-one with the great man and then Chislenko swept past Facchetti and blasted a left-foot shot beyond Enrico Albertosi. And that was how it finished. Italy coach Edmondo Fabbri was under pressure – but when is an Italy coach not under pressure? Their next game was against North Korea, though, the 500-1 outsiders, so what was there to worry about?

There were 17,829 at Ayresome for what turned out to be one of the biggest shocks in World Cup history. "We did not think of winning, only of doing our best," Pak Doo-ik recalled. The Italians didn't seem to think of much at all. Assistant coach Ferruccio Valcareggi had watched North Korea's games and reported that they were "*una squadra di Ridolini*", the Italian equivalent of Fred Karno's Army or the Keystone Cops.

Faced with a team whose speed and stamina were so far the only things that had impressed anyone (though not Valcareggi,

clearly), Fabbri bizarrely chose to field a collection of his slowest defenders in combination with the midfielder Giacomo Bulgarelli, who was struggling to shrug off the effects of a knee injury picked up against Chile. After 30 uneventful minutes it was Bulgarelli who made the game's first telling act, launching himself at Pak Seung-jin from behind. The Korean bounced back up after the foul, but the Italian lay on the deck in agony, his knee ligaments torn.

Down to 10 men against opponents who harried and chased remorselessly, Italy wilted. The Koreans (or "The little men from north of the 38th parallel" as the *Guardian*'s David Lacey liked to style them – there were many epithets for them but a reference to their diminutive size seemed compulsory) were so committed that when one of them, Han Bong-jin, collided with a corner flag he snapped it in half. "Korea, Korea," chanted the crowd, sensing sensation. In the 42nd minute an Italian clearance was headed back into the penalty area and Pak Doo-ik drilled a low shot past Albertosi. There was no way back for Italy.

On Teesside Pak Doo-ik (often said to be a dentist, though in fact he was a printer, the confusion arising from the fact that Italian papers nicknamed him "the dentist" because of the pain he inflicted) became a local hero, his name familiar to generations not old enough to have seen him play. Middlesbrough director Charles Amer invited the North Koreans to his stately home, Normanby Hall, for tea and scones and presented each of them with a Churchill crown (25p in the new money).

The barman at the team hotel confirmed rumours that the North Korea players had celebrated with a session of heavy drinking, "Oh aye," he said, "the North Koreans drunk us dry. There was no soda water left at all." Maybe so, but their sports minister seems to have been less abstemious. At a dinner hosted by Middlesbrough FC, he communicated his disappointment at being served only red wine with the meal through an interpreter, asking for Drambuie instead. According to reports he polished off a bottle and a half during the evening before demanding another bottle of the liqueur to take to bed. "Now that's what I call drinking in any language," Charlie Amer would later concede admiringly.

As the Koreans celebrated, the Italians flew back to Genoa and a hail of rotten tomatoes. "I was pretty quick in those days," Sandro Mazzola would recall wryly, "so none hit me." Fabbri was sacked, Janich, Perani and Barison dumped from the team for good. Shamed by the display, Italy's FA banned the importation of foreign players, scuppering a £500,000 deal that would have taken Eusébio to Roma.

In the final game the Soviet Union, already through thanks to Italy's implosion, sent out a virtual second team. Chile might have gone through if they had won, but their finishing was hopeless and the oddly named Valery Porkujan broke away to score twice as his team maintained their 100 per cent record with a 2-1 win at Roker Park in front of only 16,027.

In Sunderland, there had been some trepidation that their quarter-final might feature Italy and Brazil. As a contest it would have been a highlight, as a logistical problem a nightmare. Both teams had large travelling bands of supporters and, as earlier experiences had shown, the local infrastructure was hardly geared for mass tourism. Luckily the two glamour teams had gone home early, so there was no need to appeal for spare rooms. A crowd of just 22,103 watched the USSR take on Hungary.

The game was nothing to write home about either, unless your parents happened to be specialists in goalkeeping errors. Hungary took a physical battering from the Soviets, who clearly felt brutality was the best way to combat Ferenc Bene and Flórián Albert [see North West section]. But in the end the Magyars' main problem was

József Gelei, who pretty much defined the word hapless. After just five minutes he collected a cross from Porkujan only to immediately drop it right at the feet of Chislenko, who poked the ball home. Gelei knelt and apparently offered up a prayer, but God was clearly on the side of the big battalions. Two minutes into the second half the Hungary goalie fumbled a Galimzyan Khusainov free-kick, letting in Porkujan. Hungary pressed remorselessly and pulled a goal back through Bene, but failed to find the net again. Yashin saved brilliantly from a Ferenc Sipos free-kick to rub salt in Hungary's self-inflicted wound.

And for the north-east that was the end of the party. There was talk that the World Cup had been a failure in the region, something that the FA and the organizers strongly denied. Certainly the crowds had been poor, but not as bad as they had been

in Chile, where the average attendances at group stage matches at several venues had been fewer than 10,000. Then again, ticket prices in Chile were higher and the local population poorer. Whatever, the liaison committee in Sunderland pronounced the whole thing a huge success. "The town has been placed on the world map in an attractive manner and its reputation enhanced," they concluded, which in those days was as near to whooping and waving your arms about as it got.

For Middlesbrough, too, the tournament had been a success, thanks largely to the North Koreans. A strange and powerful bond was forged and to this day the north-east town is better known in Pyongyang than London is. "The English people took us to their hearts and vice versa," said Pak Doo-ik. For once, sport really had brought people closer together.

A British sailor parades around Ayresome Park, Middlesbrough, with North Korea's Kim Seung-il after the 1-1 draw with Chile on 15 July
Ron Bell/ Johnny Horton, Press Association

**The North Koreans expose
themselves to Western culture in the
form of a Laurel and Hardy film at
their Teesside hotel, the St George**
BIPPA Photo Pool

Previous page The Italians stride across the tarmac at Newcastle airport on 7 July after flying up from London. At the front on the far left is captain Giacinto Facchetti
Sunderland Echo

Han Bong-jin troops through the long grass around the North Koreans' hotel and training pitch at Middleton near Darlington
Syndication International

At Roker Park on 4 July, Sunderland
players Colin Suggett and Derek
Forster inspect the wire-mesh tunnel
required by Fifa for World Cup venues
Sunderland Echo

Alterations take place in the dressing
rooms at Ayresome Park to bring
them up to World Cup standards
Bob Dear, Associated Press

By 25 July the World Cup has moved
on and temporary seating placed over
the terraces is removed at Roker Park
Sunderland Echo

Lev Yashin is the
centre of attention
as he assesses the
biscuit selection at
Thorney Close youth
centre, Sunderland
Sunderland Echo

Yashin is in demand
again before his
team's first game,
at Ayresome Park
against North Korea
BIPPA Photo Pool

Chile's Honorino Landa is helped out of the Roker Park crowd. The South Americans lost their final game to the Soviet Union who, already through as group winners, fielded a reserve side
Tom Buist/Mirror

As North East group winners, the Soviet
Union team remain in Sunderland for the
quarter-final with Hungary
Top A game of snooker helps pass the
time for Vladimir Ponomarev (at the
table) and Anatoly Banishevsky
BIPPA Photo Pool
Bottom New boots arrive for Galimzyan
Khusainov (left) and Murtaz Khurtsilava
Keystone

Soviet players Eduard Malofeyev,
Vladimir Ponomarev and Iosif Sabo
line up at Ayresome Park for their
opening group game, against
North Korea on 12 July
Ron Bell, Press Association

Top left **The Hungarians stretch out on arrival at Sunderland for their quarter-final with the USSR**
Sunderland Echo

Top right **Giovanni Lodetti and his Italy team-mates take a more relaxed approach**
BIPPA Photo Pool

Bottom left **Galimzyan Khusainov (left) and Eduard Malofeyev train at Ayresome Park, watched by Soviet Union coach Nikolai Morozov**
Sunderland Echo

Bottom right **The North Koreans play leapfrog in training near Middleton**
BIPPA Photo Pool

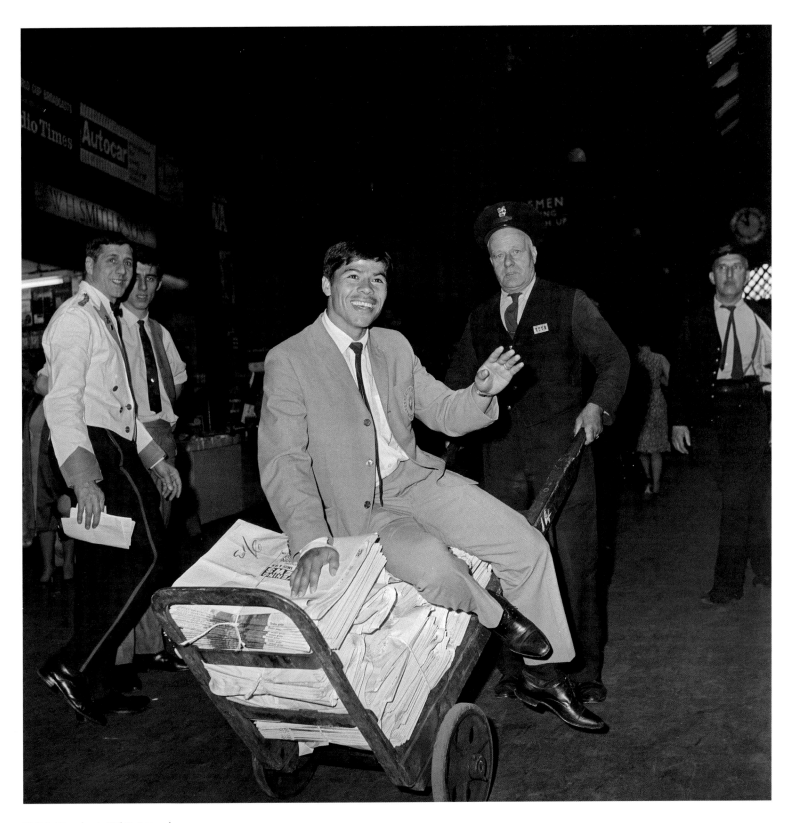

Chile's Humberto "Chita" Cruz hops
on a porter's trolley at King's Cross
en route to Newcastle
BIPPA Photo Pool

Previous page Valery Porkujan (right) scored twice against Chile after being drafted in by the Soviet Union for their final match, with qualification secure. He kept his place in the team and scored twice more in the knockout stages. The *Mirror* photographer noted "the light was not good, there was a 'sea-fret' according to the locals"
Sunderland Echo

Below left The Chile players stretch their limbs as they wait to shake hands with the Minister for Sport, Denis Howell, before their opening match, against Italy at Roker Park on 13 July
Below right The Italy players do likewise
Ron Bell, Press Association

Chile's Armando Tobar is carried off during the game against Italy, which his team lost 2-0

An over-enthusiastic Chilean
photographer is removed from the
Roker Park pitch by a policeman after
Chile equalize against the Soviet
Union in their 2-1 defeat on 20 July
Tom Buist, Mirror

A policeman keeps a more distant eye
from the terraces at Gateshead's
Redheugh Park ground, as Chile train
BIPPA Photo Pool

Tickets sales do a decent trade at a
spartan-looking Roker Park on 11 July
Sunderland Echo

Jeanette Arkle and Kathleen Riddell
with a mascot, customized by Roker
Park cafe owner Peter Crawford for a
World Cup window display
Northern Echo

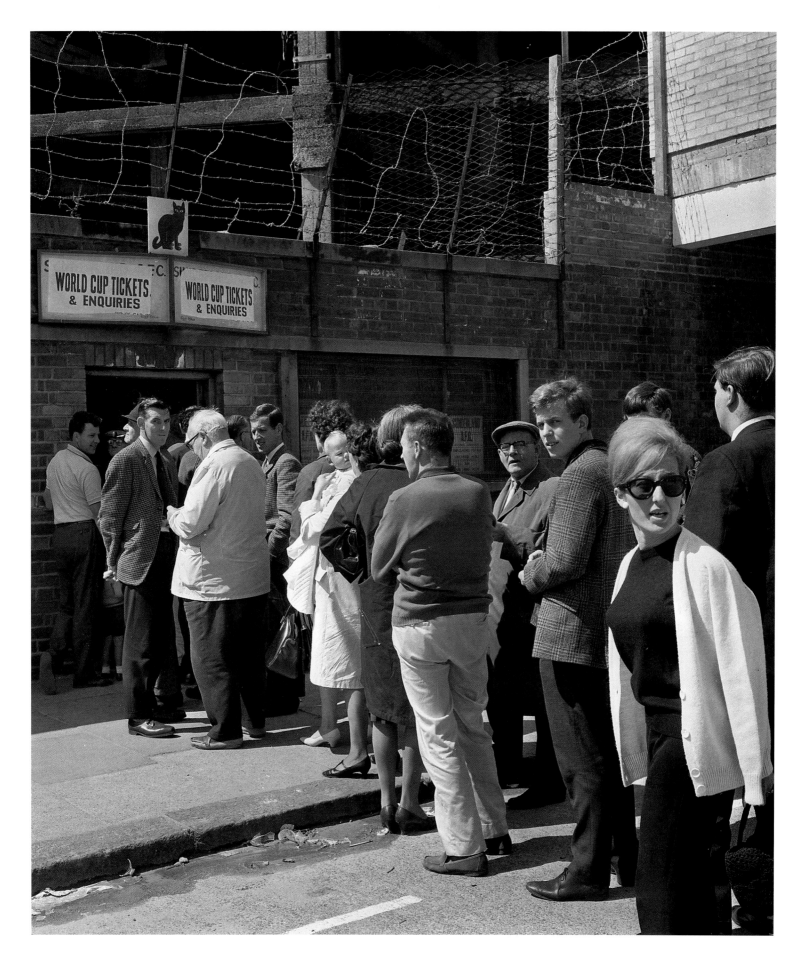

The Italians take lunch in the
customized refectory at their
residence, the School of Agriculture,
Houghall, Durham. Giacomo
Bulgarelli pours the water
BIPPA Photo Pool

Italy squad members familiarize themselves with the locale
Top left Tentatively agreeing to requests to feed the cows
Top right Gianni Rivera picks up a handheld plough with a distinct lack of confidence

Bottom left A wander through the streets of Durham, with the towering Giacinto Facchetti on the right
Bottom right Facchetti and Tarcisio Burgnich try a speculative hand at rowing on the Wear
BIPPA Photo Pool

**A Soviet fan in high spirits before
the quarter-final against Hungary
in Sunderland on 23 July**
Andre Lecoq/Robert Legros, L'Equipe

**Lev Yashin saves a shot from Italy's
Sandro Mazzola in the Soviet Union's
1-0 win at Roker Park on 16 July**
Ron Bell/Johnny Horton,
Press Association

A wet night in Sunderland for all
concerned, including youngsters
huddled against the front rail, as
Italy attack the Chile goal on 13 July

John Varley, Mirror

Above **Sándor Mátrai falls over the pitch barrier during Hungary's quarter-final against the Soviet Union at Roker Park on 23 July**
Tom Buist, Mirror

Italy manager Edmondo Fabbri faces
his critics at the press conference
following his team's shock elimination
by North Korea
BIPPA Photo Pool

Fabbri stands with head bowed
alongside Artemio Franchi, the
vice-president of the Italian Football
Federation. The manager was sacked
on his return to Italy, after dodging the
obligatory rotten tomatoes thrown by
enraged supporters at Genoa airport
BIPPA Photo Pool

The Soviet Union
press the Italians
in front of the
packed Roker
End, Sunderland
John Varley/
Tom Buist, Mirror

Chile's Rubén Marcos shares a ride with Ronnie Roughead, an 11-year-old from Gateshead
BIPPA Photo Pool

The press agency caption written at the time reads: "Only half the Russians [sic] were training on Monday while the others took turkish baths. The Russians invited two local lads who were watching to come on to the pitch and charge their goalkeeper Kavazashvili in practise [sic]. The two boys are Greg Walsh, 17 of Durham, and Stuart Fitzgerald, 19 of Newcastle. Both work for the GPO"
BIPPA Photo Pool

Soviet players (from left) Georgy
Sichinava, Alex Korneev and Victor
Getmanov at Jack Brown's barbers in
Durham on 8 July. While some squad
members opted for styles in the manner
of Napoleon Solo (Robert Vaughn's
character from spy series *The Man From
U.N.C.L.E.*) or the singer Perry Como,
Korneev chose a Dick van Dyke
Sunderland Echo

Well groomed and strolling out
ratpack style from their residence at
Grey College, Durham
Sunderland Echo

**Paolo Barison of Italy scores the
second goal in their 2-0 win against
Chile at Roker Park on 13 July**
Syndication International

Lee Chan-myung can't keep out
Rubén Marcos's penalty, but North
Korea would equalize with two

Left Italian supporters enjoy their team's 2-0 win against Chile at Roker Park on 13 July
Below More fans make their arrival known on Sunderland's Wear Bridge. The local paper reported that they were a group of waiters – from Keswick in Cumberland
Sunderland Echo

**A famous picture that sums up the
efforts of the North Koreans to protect
their narrow lead. Shin Yung-kyoo and
Giacinto Facchetti jump the highest**
BIPPA Photo Pool

**Pak Doo-ik has scored against Italy
on 19 July to enter football folklore.
Pak Seung-jin gleefully follows the ball
into the net and North Korea flags are
waved in the Ayresome Park crowd**
Ron Bell/Johnny Horton, Press Association

Jubilant North Korea players leave the pitch after their historic win over Italy. The player third left is the goalscorer Pak Doo-ik. The grey-coated officials join the celebrations, furthest right is coach Yun Seung-chul

Ron Bell, Press Association

1966
MIDLANDS

There may have been howls of protest in Yorkshire, but for the purpose of Group Two of the World Cup it was decided that Sheffield should be in the Midlands. This allowed the pairing of two of England's larger stadiums and regular FA Cup semi-final venues, Villa Park and Hillsborough – where the fateful Leppings Lane End, scene of the 1989 disaster, was built specifically for the tournament.

Like all English grounds these venues, the FA noted in their official report with a slight air of superiority, lacked the moats and high fences that were regarded as a necessity in more volatile lands. The arrival of fans from across the globe therefore made extensive preparations necessary. "It was pointed out that while English crowds were unlikely to be highly partisan, national emotions might run high in matches in which competing teams were watched by large numbers of their own nationals."

Fearing a possible outbreak of distinctly un-English offences including "the throwing of streamers, blowing of whistles by spectators and the discharge of fireworks", the committee consulted senior police officers and outlined a sweeping range of security measures, which included covering the players' tunnels with steel mesh, ensuring that all drinks in the ground were served in cardboard containers and that supporters of different nationalities would be kept in different parts of the ground "as far as possible". To help maintain discipline the FA called for a small army of voluntary stewards. Motivated by a mix of civic duty and the chance to watch football for free three times, more people came forward than were actually needed.

As well as crowds, the World Cup venues were also preparing themselves for the invasion of another potentially unruly mob – the world's media. In total 2158 press, photographers, radio and television accreditations had been issued, to people from 62 countries, including Luxembourg,

Tunisia, Mauritius and Sudan. Sixty radio organizations (including 11 from Brazil) would be broadcasting live from the grounds, while TV images would be beamed to 69 stations around the world.

Most English grounds had press seating for 40 journalists; this had to be increased to accommodate at least 400. As if this were not problematic enough, Fifa also wanted each journalist to be provided with a work space 27 inches wide, whereas the FA at that time only allowed the hacks 18 inches of writing room. The new Goodison Park press box held 120 reporters, but for the semi-final this had to be increased to 700. "This is the first report I have ever filed from a mousehole," a Swedish journalist wrote sardonically after that game.

The larger number of reporters (then filing not only by phone but also via telex and telegram) placed a strain on telecommunications facilities that had to be augmented with a new underground cable at a cost of £10,000. The number of telephones in the press centres seems strangely low, with just 210 communal phones spread across all the venues, though many news organizations booked private lines in the stadiums themselves.

By today's standards the telex is a vast and unwieldy machine, but in 1966 it was the latest innovation and proved hugely popular, particularly with Italian, German and South American journalists. The longest telex sent during the tournament was dispatched from the Birmingham press centre (in the University of Aston) to Buenos Aires. It measured 35 feet and cost the newspaper in question £315.

There were 172 photographers covering the tournament. The numbers resulted in the introduction of new rules and regulations. Only 20 were allowed into provincial grounds, 27 at Wembley. For the first time, the use of cameras was forbidden in the dressing rooms after the game. In previous World Cups photographers had

been allowed to roam along the touchlines at will. Now they were confined to two designated areas behind the goals and given a strict warning about not running on to the field while games were in play.

Not that they were going to find it all that easy to place their photographs with the British press. Sport was kept firmly in its place at the back of the newspapers and generally confined to a maximum of four pages, one of which was more or less completely devoted to horse racing. In serious newspapers such as the *Times* it was lucky to get even that. The Thunderer had refrained from covering professional football until the early 1950s, preferring to concentrate its attention on games involving the gentlemen amateurs of Pegasus and Corinthian Casuals and matches between the public schools.

On the day of the tournament's opening game, the *Daily Express* log shows snappers being dispatched to photograph Miss

Switzerland prepare for their game against Argentina on 19 July, the last of their three defeats at Hillsborough
Photopress Archiv

Gabrielle Wren "who was in a car crash with Prince Richard of Gloucester", schoolboys at Eton College on motorcycles, Neil Willson "polevaulter, walks across London carrying two poles", Rudolf Nureyev, Cyd Charisse, Hector Naylor "70 yr old cricketer" and Jennifer McHarg "a blind girl who is going to East Africa to teach – she is 25 yrs old". World Cup photographs, meanwhile, amounted to two of the England team and one of the Uruguay captain, Horacio Troche.

Group Two contained three teams – Argentina, West Germany and Spain – with at least notional chances of carrying off the main prize. Argentina had a team of big, tough and talented players. At sweeper, Roberto Perfumo had the unruffled yet lethal air of a trained assassin, while full-back Silvio Marzolini had fabulous close control and a range of passes that drew praise from Bobby Charlton. The 6ft 3in captain Antonio Rattín marshalled midfield and attempted something similar with the match officials; up front was Luis Artime, nicknamed *El Buon Mozo*, "the Handsome One". The mixture of skill and physical presence marked them out as potential winners of a tournament that always seemed likely to favour teams that could bludgeon as well as mesmerize their

opponents and many tipped Argentina as a good outside bet.

Spain's star was the suave and elegant Luis Suárez, the creative playmaker in Helenio Herrera's ultra-cautious Internazionale team, winners of the European Cup in 1964 and 1965. Suárez had the oiled and golden looks of a film star and earned a comparable salary. He found himself ensconced, alongside his team-mates, in a hotel in Sutton Coldfield.

Despite the success of Real Madrid and the wealth of Barcelona, Spain's record in World Cups was comparatively modest (though better than that of England, obviously). They were reigning European champions (though that title carried less prestige than it does today) and then as now generally came into tournaments tagged as "potential dark horses", only to leave early after revealing themselves as old nags. Spain had only scraped through to the 1966 finals via a 1-0 play-off win over the Republic of Ireland after the only other team in the group, Syria, had withdrawn.

In their match at Villa Park, Spain were easy prey for an Argentina side that masterfully mixed ball-skills, swift, neat passing and defending that leaned towards the granite-like. When Suárez tried to create something for his side by advancing on goal he was battered to the ground. His only real contribution came with a cross that the Argentina goalkeeper Antonio Roma – whose arms were so long they seemed to reach to his knees – slapped into his own net under pressure from Pirri. The Spaniard is usually credited with the goal. The watching England players, who had marked out Argentina as likely quarter-final opponents, went away impressed.

Switzerland were handicapped for their opening game, against West Germany, by internal suspensions handed to Werner Leimgruber and Jakob Kuhn. The pair had arrived back at the Hallam Tower Hotel after the evening curfew. They claimed they

had got lost while sight-seeing in Sheffield, but this failed to convince their manager, Alfredo Foni. He had played in Italy's 1938 World Cup-winning side and, despite the fact that his charges were amateurs, took a strictly professional view of breaches of discipline. Even with their two best players in the side it seems unlikely Switzerland could have coped with West Germany. Without them, they ended up conceding as many goals (three) in the first 40 minutes as they had done in six qualifying matches and eventually lost 5-0. A poor outcome for one Swiss fan, who had walked all the way from Zurich pushing his belongings in a pram to watch them.

The Germans were not yet the World Cup-dominating behemoths they would later become. They were rated as long as 33-1 shots to win the tournament, odds that would be inconceivable today, but their side was excellent. Franz Beckenbauer was still a youthful prodigy; Wolfgang Overath a model of power and precision; Karl-Heinz Schnellinger of Milan an officer-class version of the traditional British centre-half.

The blond-haired Helmut Haller was a skilful playmaker gifted enough to have guided Bologna to a *Serie A* title. He had the look of the actor Hardy Kruger – and put in a fair bit of acting of his own. His reputation for histrionics was blamed on his having spent so much time in Italy; in truth, though, it seems to have owed more to his personality. He was one of the first players the English crowds had ever seen writhing about in fake agony. They took as instant a dislike to him as they would later to another creative German midfielder, Andreas Möller. Haller repaid them after the final by carrying off the matchball and keeping it in his cellar for three decades.

Up front for West Germany was the balding, ruddy-cheeked Uwe Seeler, a diminutive yet powerful centre-forward with a barrel chest and thickly muscled thighs who hurled himself into diving headers with

A news kiosk in
Sheffield extends
a welcome in
German to World
Cup visitors
Photopress Archiv

Spain fans try to generate some enthusiasm for their first group game against Argentina at Villa Park on 13 July. Spain lost 2-1

Ron Viner, Express
©Getty Images

so little thought for the damage he might sustain that it's as if he was joy-riding a stolen body. Seeler was nicknamed "the Hamburg Torpedo", which sounds like something you might buy in a shop on the Reeperbahn, and, despite having recently had an artificial Achilles tendon installed, he led the line with combative swagger.

West Germany's manager was Helmut Schön, who had scored Dresdner SC's winning goal in the last German Cup final before D-Day. On the bench, Schön favoured a combination of checked flat cap and tracksuit. Crumple-faced and amiable, he appeared to command the respect of his players through the sheer benign force of his personality, a Teutonic Bob Paisley.

People looking for weaknesses in the German line-up pointed to the fact that Lothar Emmerich wasn't quick enough to be an international winger, that the chubby Haller tended to tire and that goalkeeper Hans Tilkowski was suspect, though the fact that the Borussia Dortmund man had been voted German footballer of the year in 1965 suggested he was no Gary Sprake.

At Hillsborough there was little sign of fragility. The best elements of Schön's team combined wonderfully and the Swiss were brushed aside in front of a crowd of 36,000 that included nearly 10,000 German fans, at least 2000 of whom seemed to be armed with banners or brass instruments.

Against Switzerland, Spain began nervously. With Kuhn and Leimgruber restored to their ranks alongside the country's most expensive player, Heinz Schneitter of Young Boys, the Swiss surprisingly spent most of the first half on the attack and scored through René-Pierre Quentin. At half-time something seems to have come over both teams. The Spanish returned inspired, the Swiss nervy and defensive. In the 57th minute Spain defender Manuel Sanchís ran half the length of the field while the opposing defenders looked on mesmerized and he finished with a dinky chip over the goalkeeper. Then, after Quentin had had a goal surprisingly disallowed by the Russian referee, Francisco Gento ("The fastest player I've ever seen," said Bobby Charlton,

speaking of an earlier incarnation) gave a glimpse of the old magic. The Real Madrid winger had previously been standing on the touchline looking like a portly ballboy, but now burst into life and crossed for Amaro Amancio to dive full length and head home the second in a 2-1 win.

Despite another partisan crowd, the Germans could make little headway against Argentina at Villa Park and the game gradually dissolved into the sort of brutal contest that was only likely to be resolved by a submission or a knockout. In terms of both football and fighting West Germany were stronger, but Argentina had more tricks. Both sides committed nasty fouls, with Schnellinger and the tall and stick-thin Willi Schulz excelling in that department for the Germans. Argentina's Rafael Albrecht (widely regarded as the least skilful player in their line-up) was booked for bringing down Haller with a tackle worthy of one of rugby union's Pumas and was then dismissed for kneeing Wolfgang Weber in the groin. In truth, playing with 10 or 11 men made little difference in the mayhem. Marzolini played brilliantly in defence as the Germans lost their discipline and sense of purpose in a cacophony of blaring air-horns and chants of "Uwe! Uwe!" The nearest they came to scoring was when Perfumo headed against his own bar and the game petered out as a 0-0 draw.

Argentina, though, had had their card marked. There was a warning from Fifa to moderate their behaviour and "play in a more sporting manner in future games". Thousands of noisy German fans attended their next match – against Switzerland at Hillsborough – just to give Argentina the bird. The Swiss were almost as abject as they had been in their opening match, however, and surrendered 2-0. Argentina would meet England at Wembley.

Spain needed to beat West Germany at Villa Park to progress. But the golden boy Suárez was out injured, while Gento had been dropped by manager José Villalonga, who had finally noticed that he was not quite as quick as he once was, alerted perhaps by the moss growing on his north side. Despite, or perhaps because of, the absence of the two ageing stars, Spain looked much sharper and more vigorous. They took the lead through José María Fusté, who latched on to Adelardo Rodríguez's through ball and chipped Hans Tilkowski. German protests that Fusté had used his hand were ignored: the goal stood. Stung by the injustice of it all, Schön's team increased their tempo and equalized when Borussia Dortmund winger Emmerich – the *Bundesliga*'s top scorer in the previous season, but only playing now because Haller was rested – chased a loose ball down near the goalline and smashed it into the roof of the net with his left foot from a position that pretty much defined the term "impossible angle". Seeler got the winner, neatly slotting in Sigi Held's cross.

By the time of the "Midlands" quarter-final, the view that the Europeans had ganged up on the South Americans was rapidly gaining momentum, at least in South America. Argentina had suffered in their quarter-final against England thanks to a German referee, and now Uruguay [see *London section*] were taking on West Germany at Hillsborough in a match refereed by an Englishman. As if to prove a point, they ended the game with even fewer men on the field than their neighbours had.

The game started promisingly for the South Americans. They were denied an opening goal in the third minute only by the brilliance of Tilkowski, who dived full length to save a 35-yard shot from Julio César Cortés that the correspondent from the *Daily Telegraph* likened to an exploding shell and they continued to press even after the Germans took the lead with a freak goal – Held's long-range shot deflecting in off an apparently oblivious Haller.

In the second half, the mood was altered irrevocably when the referee, James Finney, turned aside Uruguayan penalty appeals after Schnellinger clearly stopped the ball on the line with his arm. Aggrieved by what they saw as another example of a European referee favouring a European team, Uruguay took the law into their own hands. Violence broke out everywhere. Emmerich hacked the opposing skipper Horacio Troche, who responded by kicking him in the stomach. Dismissed, Troche stomped off, pausing only to deliver a sharp slap to the cheek of Uwe Seeler, who burst out laughing more in shock than amusement. Minutes later Héctor Silva kicked Schulz as Tilkowski collected the ball and then ran through and whacked the keeper, following up this double by stamping on Haller who – as usual – was prostrate with agony. Finney sent off the Uruguayan.

Initially, like Antonio Rattín in Argentina's match with England, Silva refused to go and after finally being hustled to the touchline was surrounded by a quartet of policemen who appeared on the verge of giving him a good going-over with their truncheons when he finally calmed down. With only nine players left and their discipline lost completely, Uruguay caved in. Beckenbauer scored a lovely goal, running away in his trademark languid manner after being put through by Seeler. The Torpedo added the third from 18 yards, prompting a pitch invasion from a portly, flag-waving German in *lederhosen*, and Haller added the finishing touch after a mistake by Jorge Manicera.

The police escort Yugoslav referee Konstantin Zecevic off the pitch at Villa Park, after the acrimonious 0-0 draw between Argentina and West Germany on 16 July in which the South Americans had Rafael Albrecht dismissed
BIPPA Photo Pool

Flags are handed out to fans to drum
up support for the already eliminated
Swiss team before their final game,
against Argentina at Hillsborough on
19 July. It didn't work: they lost 2-0
Photopress Archiv

A 7ft floral football is constructed
and unveiled in Victoria Square,
Birmingham. The "living football",
built by six parks department
gardeners, comprised more than
8000 plants
Birmingham Post & Mail

Sepp Herberger, West Germany's manager for their legendary 1954 World Cup triumph and an adviser to Helmut Schön in 1966, talks to the press. Watching from the bus is reserve goalkeeper Sepp Maier, a World Cup winner in 1974
Willi Gutberlet, DPA

Top Franz Beckenbauer trains at the Recreation Ground, the home of Ashbourne Town in Derbyshire. Ashbourne is home of one of England's historic Shrove Tuesday football matches, involving hundreds of people playing through the town centre
Andre Lecoq/Robert Legros, L'Equipe

Bottom At the team hotel, the former Manchester City goalkeeper Bert Trautmann, an adviser to the squad, has breakfast with manager Helmut Schön
BIPPA Photo Pool

Previous page Argentina's Oscar Más (left) makes a flying but unsuccessful effort to direct a header at the Swiss goal, evading defender Xavier Stierli in their final group game at Hillsborough on 19 July
Reg Bagnall/Denis Evans, Press Association

Argentina goalkeeper Antonio Roma checks the height of one of the crossbars at Villa Park, venue for their group games against Spain and West Germany, in a pre-tournament inspection on 5 July
Reg Bagnall, Press Association

Argentina captain Antonio Rattín was absent from the team's inspection of Villa Park, the local press reported, having woken up with toothache
Gerry Armes, Birmingham Post & Mail

Silvio Marzoloni (left) and Antonio Roma assist Birmingham chef John Brownlees in preparing steaks for the Argentine Independence Day barbecue to be held at the Tally Ho! police training centre
Gerry Armes, Birmingham Post & Mail

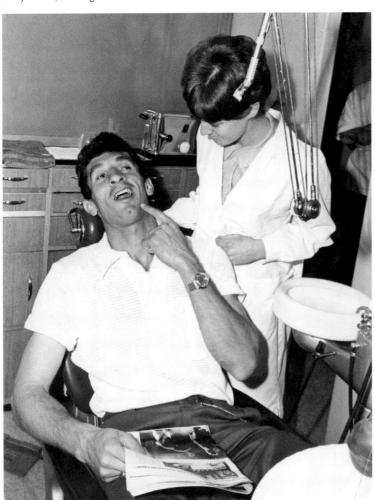

Wolfgang Weber gets to grips with a biro as he signs autographs for West German fans, equipped with an impressive array of camera equipment, at Villa Park
BIPPA Photo Pool

From left to right, on 7 July Spain's Manuel Sanchís, Gallego, Miguel Reina and Luis Del Sol find a card game the best way to cope with the excitement of arriving in England
BIPPA Photo Pool

Amaro Amancio, scorer of Spain's winning goal against Switzerland at Hillsborough, signs autographs in Birmingham on 17 July
BIPPA Photo Pool

Switzerland goalkeeper Karl Elsener
dives to save at the feet of Spain's
Joaquín Peiró as Werner Leimgruber,
recalled after a suspension for
breaking curfew, looks on at
Hillsborough on 15 July
Reg Bagnall/Denis Evans,
Press Association

The stadium scoreboard after Spain's 2-1 win against Switzerland at Hillsborough. The result left the Swiss with the slimmest of hopes for survival and it was goodnight for both teams at the end of the group stage

Photopress Archiv

Top Delta Metal Co in Erdington, Birmingham, prepare to welcome the Spain team to the works' sports ground
Birmingham Post & Mail
Bottom Fritz Walter, captain of West Germany's 1954 World Cup winners, visits the Spain team before their game against his compatriots, carrying a copy of the Jules Rimet trophy
BIPPA Photo Pool

Despite distractions to the far right, the Spain players take in some advice, presumably from the owner of the finger that is pointing into the picture, also on the right
BIPPA Photo Pool

Posters to promote the matches to be
played at Sheffield Wednesday's
ground go up in June 1966
Reg Bagnall, Press Association

A giant football gets finishing touches
before readied for hoisting on to a 25ft
pole at the corner of New Street and
Corporation Street in Birmingham,
while a mystery hand bangs a nail in
the "C" of cup
Birmingham Post & Mail

**A Swiss flag is added to those on
display in Sheffield**
Photopress Archiv

Fans make use of flags to take shelter
from the July weather at Hillsborough
before Switzerland's game with Spain
on 15 July
BIPPA Photo pool

A supporter dresses up to commemorate West Germany's 1954 World Cup win and express his hopes for a repeat in 1966
BIPPA Photo Pool

Franz Beckenbauer and the rest of the West Germany squad make themselves at home at the Peveril of the Peak hotel in Derbyshire, named after a novel by Sir Walter Scott
Top Checking into his room with room-mate Helmut Haller
Bottom World Cup Willie stops by for tea and cakes

Top A tour of the kitchen with Haller and team chef Hans Damker
Bottom A look at the peaks with an unimpressed Uwe Seeler
BIPPA Photo Pool

Previous page Franz Beckenbauer
(No 4) celebrates with his team-mates
after scoring West Germany's second
goal in their fractious 4-0 quarter-final
win against Uruguay at Hillsborough
on 23 July
John Varley, Mirror

Below left Swiss players take a brief
stroll outside the confines of their
training ground and hotel in Sheffield
BIPPA Photo Pool
Below right Their fans do likewise
around the city centre
Photopress Archiv

The sight-seeing
bus tours of
Birmingham go
multilingual
Birmingham
Post & Mail

**Spain players chew hard as they take a
look around Villa Park**
Gerry Armes, Birmingham Post & Mail

Argentina celebrate after their 2-1
victory against Spain at Villa Park
on 13 July. Luis Artime, the scorer of
both his side's goals, is grabbed
round the neck by a team-mate
BIPPA Photo Pool

Top The usual crop of enthusiastic youngsters watch the Germans at their Derbyshire base
Bottom René Brodmann of Switzerland plays leap frog with team-mates in training at Abbeydale Sports Ground, Sheffield
BIPPA Photo Pool

Top Spain's Francisco Gento takes a break from ballwork
Bottom Antonio Rattín (right) goes shoulder to shoulder with José Varacka as Argentina work out
BIPPA Photo Pool

Left Pablo Forlán of Uruguay at Hillsborough before his side's quarter-final against West Germany. His son, Diego, plays for his country today
Reg Bagnall/Denis Evans, Press Association

**Sunbathers look on as balls fly
while West Germany train for their
quarter-final against Uruguay**
Reg Bagnall/Denis Evans,
Press Association

Edward Holliger, who walked from
Zurich to watch the Swiss, collected
gifts on the way in a pram – as well as
incredulous looks from the locals
BIPPA Photo Pool

A Spain fan brings a dash of colour to Villa Park. He appears to be the only Spaniard in among the neutrals and a scattering of West Germany fans for the game on 20 July
BIPPA Photo Pool

Top A pitch invader joins the players in saluting a West Germany goal against Spain in their 2-1 win
Bottom Nursing staff enjoy a goal from the same game. Sigi Held (left) and Lothar Emmerich celebrate
Hans-Dietrich Kaiser, Nordbild

The balding Helmut Schön leads his
squad's training at Ashbourne in
Derbyshire on 11 July, the eve of their
first game. In qualifiers for the 1954
World Cup, Schön had coached the
then independent state of Saar – not
united with West Germany until 1957
– against his future employers
BIPPA Photo Pool

Trainer Udo Lattek, manager Helmut Schön and Franz Beckenbauer lead West Germany off the pitch after their 2-1 victory against Spain at Villa Park on 20 July, with qualification for the knockout stages assured

Hans-Dietrich Kaiser, Nordbild

**Uruguay's Julio César Cortés (centre) and
Luis Ramos (right) are intrigued by an
accordion player as they wait to board the
team coach before their quarter-final with
West Germany on 23 July**
Reg Bagnall, Press Association

**Uruguay captain Horacio Troche
flashes a V-for-victory sign as he leads
his team out before the match at
Hillsborough. The game against West
Germany would end with somewhat
different gestures**
Reg Bagnall/Denis Evans,
Press Association

**Argentina players pass round letters
during a meal at the Albany Hotel**
Gerry Armes, Birmingham Post & Mail

A scene of jubilation in the Argentina
dressing room after the 2-1 win
against Spain at Villa Park on 13 July.
Manager Juan Carlos Lorenzo is
embraced by José Santiago, a club
delegate from Club Atlético Platense.
Photographers were banned from the
dressing rooms at the World Cup,
making this a rare picture opportunity
Jeff Heath, Birmingham Post & Mail

Uruguay coach Juan Lopez, who had been in charge of the 1950 World Cup winners, and assorted players join the fray at Hillsborough as the furore surrounding the dismissal of Héctor Silva (far left) against West Germany drags on

John Varley, Mirror

1966
NORTH WEST

Violence on the field had been a feature of past World Cups and, as luck would have it, the draw for the 1966 finals recreated two of the most notorious football matches in history – the Battle of Santiago (Italy v Chile, 1962) and, in the north-west, the Battle of Berne (Brazil v Hungary, 1954). With no substitutions and referees apparently oblivious to violent conduct of all but the most murderous sort, the fact that there was not even more foul play was surely due only to the fear of even more terrible retribution. It was dog eat dog. Fearing the worst, the Ministry of Health had declared that as visitors the players would be entitled to free treatment for "emergency conditions only" and would have to pay for anything else.

Of more immediate concern was the state of the stadiums. Old Trafford was the only ground in the country apart from Wembley that met all Fifa's specifications. The world governing body stipulated that every pitch used in the tournament must measure precisely 115 yards by 75 yards, precluding the use of many major grounds with small pitches, including Highbury. At Goodison Park, usually regarded as the second best stadium in the country, the playing area had to be lengthened by 14 feet and widened by six to meet the standards. Liverpool City Council even had to be persuaded to rehouse residents of a terrace behind the Park Stand so that it could be demolished to make way for the extension.

Such extreme measures seemed to be more than justified when the draw was made. If the term "Group of Death" had been coined it would surely have been applied to Group Three, which featured three of the best sides in the tournament in Brazil, Portugal and Hungary. Bulgaria were awkward makeweights. When the draw was made, Brazilian official Silvio Paccheto claimed: "It is a very good draw for us. We fear no one." Maybe he was putting a brave face on it, and then again maybe not.

Brazil strolled into England on the back of two consecutive World Cup wins. The administration of the CBF, their FA, gave the impression that to claim a third all they had to do was turn up. The party was selected as if for a victory parade, with ageing and injured players all picked less on current ability than for past glories. Two, the defenders Orlando and Bellini, had been left out in 1962 because they were thought too old. Manager Vicente Feola, tubby, with heavy jowls and moist eyes that gave his face a perpetual air of melancholy, had a life-threatening heart condition.

Fittingly, perhaps, the squad's preparations in Brazil were played out against a backdrop of fireworks, banquets and civic receptions – as if they had already returned victorious. Despite spending three months together, the players hardly seemed to get to train at all. But if the FA and public were blind to the situation, the coaches were not. Sent on a scouting mission to Europe, Ernesto Santos returned to report that in terms of fitness, tactics and teamwork England, West Germany, Hungary and Portugal were all superior to Brazil. "We'll need a miracle if we're to win the cup again," he concluded grimly.

On the other hand, Brazil did have the world's greatest player. Just the thought of Pelé sent most football writers into a spin. Purnell's *World Cup 1966 England* ("A Publication Officially Approved By The Football Association") noted breathlessly that Pelé's annual income was "estimated at something in the region of £75,000", though "he probably doesn't know what he earns himself". Given the great man's later financial problems, this statement was probably more accurate than they realized.

Brazil were based at Lymm in Cheshire. Unable to speak English, the players fell prey to the sort of paranoia that traditionally grips the British abroad. Somebody told them it was unsafe to walk the streets after dark, so they all – including that inveterate

The Goodison Park crowd during the semi-final between West Germany and the Soviet Union on 25 July, protesting at Fifa's decision to schedule England's semi, like all their other games, at Wembley
Eric Shaw/ George Stephenson, Press Association

party animal Garrincha – stayed indoors at night. The management had decided the players should room singly, rather than in the traditional pairs. Far from solitude helping the players rest, however, it only served to unsettle them further, especially when rumours went around that the hotel was haunted. When somebody whispered that the only meat the English served was horseflesh, most of the squad refused to eat anything at dinner except potatoes and cabbage. The sad-faced Feola watched it all through dark glasses, protecting his eyes from the pitiless English sun.

Around 5000 fans travelled from Brazil, bringing with them a wide selection of drums and tambourines that were initially impounded by customs and released just in time for the first match. Their chanting and syncopated clapping would change British terrace culture for ever, but it did little to increase their team's chances.

Opponents, cars smashes and alcohol had irreparably damaged Garrincha. He was the husk of the player who had terrorized left-backs in 1958 and 1962, yet João Havelange, the head of the Brazilian party, insisted that he face Bulgaria in the opening game, because in the 59 matches Pelé and the Little Bird had appeared in

Denis Howell, the
Minister of Sport,
meets the Hungary
team before their
game with Bulgaria
at Old Trafford on
20 July. Matt Busby,
the Manchester
United manager,
waits his turn on
the left
Peter Sheppard,
Mirror

together for their country Brazil had not
lost. They had lost with Garrincha. They had
lost with Pelé. But when the pair played,
history showed Brazil were unbeaten.

Bulgaria, who were in England courtesy
of a play-off win over Belgium, would
probably have been seen off without the
need for such hoodoo. But Brazil won 2-0
and Pelé and Garrincha both scored direct
from free-kicks, backing up Havelange's
theories. It was hardly an ominous display,
however, except for Brazil themselves.

From the kick-off Pelé was booted
remorselessly by his marker, Dobromir
Zhechev. There was nothing unusual about
that. Pelé was the world's greatest player, a
marked man in every sense. More
surprising was the fact that the Brazilian
didn't come up with a response. Pelé was
rightly fêted for his skills, but he was built
like a middleweight boxer, came from the
slums and had a well justified and perhaps
unsurprising reputation for being able to
look after himself. In the mini-World Cup
that had been played in 1964, he had

retaliated ferociously against the Argentina
defender José Mesiano, butting him full in
the face. Mesiano was carried off with a
broken nose. Asked if he was ever
intimidated, Pelé replied in his usual light
and charming manner: "No, because I have
never met an opponent who can hurt me
more than I can hurt him." Against
Bulgaria, apart from the odd dig with his
elbows he seemed remarkably subdued.

If Brazil had the world's greatest player,
Portugal included Europe's best, Eusébio,
the 1965 European Footballer of the Year.
Of course Eusébio da Silva Ferreira had
been born in Portuguese East Africa, what
is now Mozambique. He was the first
African footballer to gain worldwide
attention and even today, 30 years after his
retirement, it is said that of famous
Africans only Nelson Mandela is instantly
recognisable to more people.

Eusébio could run 100m in 11 seconds
(Harry Jerome of Canada had won an
Olympic bronze in 10.27 secs in 1964), had
incredible balance and could kick the ball

with such power with either foot – body
bent forward, knee practically touching
his chin – that the velocity seemed likely
to burst it. Benfica had signed him from
Sporting Club Lourenço Marques for
£7500 in 1961. Within a fortnight of
arriving he was playing at inside-left for the
Portuguese national team. The British
press dubbed him "the Black Panther".
Eusébio was initially unimpressed, fearing
the political connotations ("The Black
Panthers were a group in America who
kidnapped the heiress Patty Hearst," he
would later tell an interviewer with a
disarming lack of accuracy), but grew to be
proud of it. A deeply religious man, he
crossed himself before every game and
wore the No 13 shirt to bring him luck.

Like the Brazilians, the Portuguese
found England strange and cold. They
trained at the home of Cheadle Rovers and
lodged down the road in Wilmslow at the
Stanneylands Hotel. If the food wasn't to
their taste that didn't matter, however. They
frequently took over the hotel kitchen and,
though they had brought no specialist chef
with them, were fortunate to have, in
midfielder José Augusto, a man who could
rustle up a mean salt cod stew with hot
peppers. As if this were not enough, team
spirit was assured by the fact that no fewer
than 10 of the squad, including the entire
first-choice forward line, played for Benfica.

In their first game Portugal took on
another of the favourites, Hungary, at Old
Trafford. The Olympic champions had a
formidable team that included János
Farkas, Ferenc Bene, Flórián Albert and
the tournament's only fully qualified vet,
Dr Mate Fenyvesi. Just under 30,000 saw
Portugal win 3-1, thanks in the main to
the powerful and towering Benfica
centre-forward José Torres. At 6ft 4in, he
was one of the few men in the tournament
that Jack Charlton had to look up to.

Hungary played well, with Albert
prompting attacks from a withdrawn role

The North Korea squad
arrive at Lime Street
Station in Liverpool on
21 July. Pak Doo-ik is
the player with a ball
tucked under his arm
Peter Ralph, Sun
©Mirrorpix

Dinko Dermendjiev arrives at the Mollington Banastre Hotel in Chester on 8 July. His luggage gives a hint as to what the Bulgaria striker is there for
BIPPA Photo Pool

and István Nagy bewildering Portugal's captain, the mighty Mário Coluna (like Eusébio from Mozambique). But they lacked a real goalscorer to convert all the chances they created. The game did much to seal Hungary's fate. Not because of the result, but because of the injury inflicted on goalkeeper Antal Szentmihályi. Injured in the first minute, he was forced to stay on by the "no substitutes" rule (bad news for Eusébio, whom he accidentally punched above the left eye when lunging for a cross) and aggravated the original damage. He didn't play again. His replacement József Gelei was so accident-prone it seemed that if he put his head in his hands he'd drop it.

Against Hungary Pelé was rested, his legs still aching from the attentions of Zhechev, and time finally caught up with Garrincha and a number of his team-mates. Bellini in particular was so static it was a wonder no pigeons landed on him. The game was a classic. Hungary, inspired by a magisterial display by Albert ("Albert! Albert!" the Goodison crowd chanted, sounding the "t" in a most uncontinental fashion) who dropped deep into midfield despite the No 9 on his back, dominated for much of the game, producing mesmerizing passing and movement that still look like a

blueprint for some future style of football that has yet to emerge. At one point a move involving Rákosi, Mathesz, Mészöly, Bene and Albert saw the Hungarians exchange seven passes without the ball touching the deck, only Gylmar's save from Bene's header preventing the sequence from being hailed as the goal of the century.

They didn't ignore the more physical side of the game, either: Alcindo was taken out early and spent most of the game limping up and down the touchline. Though Brazil hung on for an hour, Hungary eventually ran out 3-1 winners. By the end the crowd were chanting: "Easy! Easy!"

It was Brazil's first World Cup defeat since 1954. If there was any comfort for them, it was that the team included in Gérson (then still sporting a full head of wavy hair), Tostão and Jairzinho the kernel of a future side of surpassing greatness.

Albert, meanwhile, left the pitch to a standing ovation, busily cooling himself down by spraying the contents of a soda siphon over his head. "There must have been dancing in the streets of Budapest when the news came through," opined Geoffrey Green in the *Times*. "Laughter even in the waters of the Danube." It was the sort of game that caused people to get carried away like that.

In front of a disappointing Old Trafford crowd of 25,438, Portugal had much less trouble with Bulgaria than Brazil had done. Eusébio dropped deep to avoid the attentions of the defenders, leaving the mighty Torres to forage alone up front, but got forward to head the second as Portugal easily triumphed 3-0.

Brazil now needed to beat Portugal. Bizarrely, coach Feola opted for wholesale changes, dropping nine players from the side that had lost to Hungary and bringing back the ageing Orlando to mark the lightning fast Eusébio. Reviewing the changes later, Pelé called them "suicidal".

Portugal were coached by a Brazilian,

Otto Glória, but there was little sentiment. Pelé, who was still carrying the bruises from the opening encounter, was put out of the game by João Morais with a vicious tackle on the edge of the penalty area that the English referee, George McCabe, apparently judged was firm but fair – maybe he thought it was Australian rules. The chunky, shaven-headed trainer-cum-masseur Mário Américo and team doctor Hilton Gosling carried Pelé from the field.

Portugal were already 2-0 up by then. Haílton Corrêa de Arruda in the Brazil goal was officially nicknamed Manga, but in honour of his pockmarked face his team-mates dubbed him Frankenstein. Boris Karloff might have done a better job with or without the bolt through his neck as the goals rained in. Eusébio ran riot, scoring with a volley from such an acute angle that it seemed to defy scientific law. Brazil were out. At the final whistle Pelé limped from the field, a bandage on his knee, a coat draped around his shoulders like a cloak, a king departing into exile.

The following day at Old Trafford, Gelei of Hungary again flapped to allow Bulgaria's centre-forward Georgi Asparoukhov to score his side's only goal of the tournament, but the nervy keeper's team-mates hit the back of the net three times so it hardly mattered. This time.

North Korea had left their billet at the Teesside airport hotel and moved to Liverpool for their quarter-final, where the accommodation arranged for them was in the Loyola Hall. This Jesuit retreat had originally been picked on the assumption that Italy would be the visitors. The collision of devout Catholicism and godless communism seemed likely to create a problem and it did – the images of tortured saints that decorated the walls so terrified the Koreans that many refused to sleep in their single rooms, preferring to bed down on the floor with their team-mates.

Going forward Portugal were formidable, but their defence was thought to be shaky and, despite the lack of shut-eye, North Korea proved it. They were a goal up in less than a minute, Pak Seung-jin shooting home from the lively Han Bong-jin's pass. Another Han Bong-jin cross then found its way right across the penalty area to Yang Sung-kook. He turned it back into the path of Lee Dong-woon, who swept it home. "We want three!" the Goodison Park crowd – swelled by several hundred supporters from Middlesbrough – chanted. They got their wish when the hero of Ayresome, Pak Doo-ik, had a shot charged down and Yang Sung-kook picked up the rebound, sidestepped a defender and slotted it past José Pereira. Just 24 minutes gone and the no-hopers led 3-0.

At this point, Eusébio appeared to get a little angry. Seizing on a through ball from José Augusto, he cracked a shot with such force he might have been intent on knocking the goalkeeper's head off. Two penalties, the first for a foul on Torres, the second when he himself was brought down, were rifled home just as emphatically. In between, his third was a mirror of the first. Job done. Later he crossed for Torres, whose header back across goal was knocked in by José Augusto. North Korea were beaten, but returned home heroes.

The semi-final at Goodison Park might have featured England and Portugal. However, the tournament rules had always allowed for the game to be switched to Wembley if England were playing in it and that's what happened. Instead of Eusébio versus Bobby Charlton, the Liverpudlians found themselves presented with the less appetising contest between West Germany and the Soviet Union.

What the game lacked in flair and finesse it made up for in raw, bludgeoning roughness, the two teams kicking and hacking so merrily it was as if they were trying to play the *William Tell Overture* on each other's shinpads. The idea that the game would end with 22 on the field was absurd. Early on Iosif Sabo whacked Franz Beckenbauer and came away limping with a twisted ankle. The rock-like Karl-Heinz Schnellinger then slid several yards to take out Igor Chislenko. The Soviet winger went off for treatment and watched from the touchline as Sigi Held roared down the pitch and hit a lovely pass into the path of Helmut Haller, who blasted it home. Incensed, the winger came back on, won the ball, lost it again and responded by kicking Held on the back of the leg. Far worse fouls had gone unpunished, but the mellifluously monikered Italian referee Concetto Lo Bello sent him off.

Beckenbauer, who – like Bobby Charlton – seems to have had a preternatural instinct for survival in the face of hostile opponents, added a second with a left-foot shot that crept in between Lev Yashin and his post. Valery Porkujan pulled a goal back for the USSR and Anatoly Banishevsky almost equalized with a header, but the Germans were clearly the better side and held on.

The Soviet coach blamed Yashin for both the goals, possibly just to cut the star player down to size a bit, because most observers felt the Soviets would have conceded a couple more if it hadn't been for the man in black. Haller said that he urinated blood for three days afterwards, the result of a series of kidney punches he suffered while waiting for corners. Poor thing. At the end of the game German fans unfurled hundred of flags, a sight that was greeted by chants of "England, England" by locals still nursing a sense of injustice over the rescheduling of the semi-finals.

Eusébio acknowledges the crowd after Portugal's epic 5-3 quarter-final victory over North Korea at Goodison Park on 23 July
Nuno Ferrari, A Bola

Policeman Sid Palmer and his Alsatian
Cindy watch the groundsman prepare
the Goodison Park pitch on 12 July,
before Brazil's game with Bulgaria
BIPPA Photo Pool

Fans at Goodison Park before the
semi-final between West Germany
and the Soviet Union on 25 July.
There's a bold attempt in the small
print at translating the golden-goal
advert into Spanish
Andre Lecoq/Robert Legros, L'Equipe

Previous page A young fan
approaches Pelé for an autograph as
he trains in the pouring rain and
patchy grass at Bolton Wanderers'
training ground on 18 July, in
preparation for Brazil's crucial match
with Portugal at Goodison Park the
next day
BIPPA Photo Pool

**Hungary train in the grounds of the
Palace Hotel in Southport on 8 July**
BIPPA Photo Pool

**Hungary, led by Dezso Molnár, arrive at
Manchester airport on 4 July, bringing
their own pitch with them**
Eric Shaw, Press Association

Portugal's team doctor, Dr João Da Silva Rocha, tends to Eusébio's injury on 15 July
Eric Shaw/George Stephenson, Press Association

Eusébio, still plastered, listens to the Old Trafford band before the game against Bulgaria on 20 July
Ernie Chapman/Peter Sheppard, Mirror

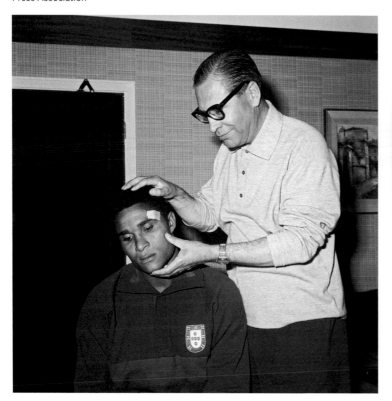

Eusébio suffers after being accidentally punched by Hungary goalkeeper Antal Szentmihályi during Portugal's 3-1 win at Old Trafford on 13 July
Eric Shaw/George Stephenson, Press Association

**Pelé takes a turn in goal during a
training session in Bolton, 17 July**
Eric Shaw, Press Association

Top Brazil try to keep the press at bay at the Lymm Hotel on 8 July, four days before their first game *Bottom* In the hotel car park, goalkeeper Gylmar seeks to draw strength from a cigarette
BIPPA Photo Pool

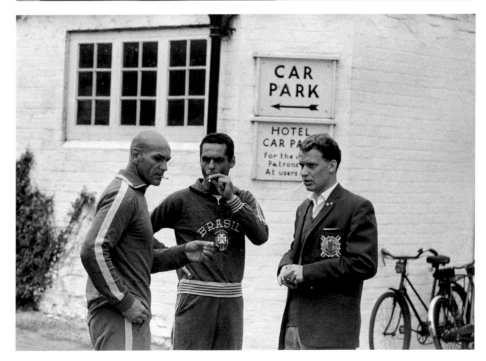

The residents of Claudia Street near
Goodison Park, Liverpool, get in the
spirit decorating their window boxes,
hanging streamers across the road
and painting kerbstones in the visiting
countries' colours
Express, Manchester edition

A street trader at Goodison Park still has plenty of rosettes for long-eliminated sides on sale on 25 July, before the Soviet Union v West Germany semi-final
Andre Lecoq/ Robert Legros, L'Equipe

Brazil fans inside Goodison Park cheer their team on against Bulgaria on 12 July – and get in some free advertising for Editora Delta SA, publishers of dictionaries and encyclopaedias
BIPPA Photo Pool

Wolfgang Weber leaps in celebration
as Helmut Haller (out of picture)
beats Lev Yashin (to right of goal),
giving West Germany the lead in their
semi-final just before half-time at
Goodison Park on 25 July
BIPPA Photo Pool

The world champions' defence gets off to a promising start at Goodison Park on 12 July, as Alcindo celebrates Pelé's 13th-minute free-kick that has given Brazil the lead against Bulgaria. The prone Georgi Naidenov has let in the first of the eight goals his country will concede in the tournament

Mirror

József Gelei, Hungary's accident-prone reserve goalkeeper (left), survives an attack by Jairzinho (right) during his side's 3-1 defeat of Brazil at Goodison Park on 15 July. English referee Ken Dagnall looks on
BIPPA Photo Pool

The North Koreans proudly inherit
the team coach kitted out for the
deposed world champions, Brazil.
Lee Dong-woon gives the World Cup
holders the thumbs down
BIPPA Photo Pool

Previous page Rudolf Vytlacil,
Bulgaria's tracksuited Austrian
coach, implores his charges to jump
higher at Manchester University's
sports ground
Eric Shaw/George Stephenson,
Press Association

The North Korea squad incongrously
check in to the convent originally
chosen for its suitability for the
Catholic tastes of the Italians.
Lim Zoong-sun (immediately beneath
the statue) observes the cleric's
kicking action
BIPPA Photo Pool

Eusébio offers consolation to the
stricken Pelé at Goodison Park.
English referee George McCabe
(centre) failed to send off the Portugal
players responsible for kicking Brazil's
star man out of the game
BIPPA Photo Pool

An angry Pelé, down and out against
Portugal, looks on in disgust during
Brazil's 3-1 defeat on 19 July. He
played on gingerly, only able to kick
with one leg
BIPPA Photo Pool

It's 13 July at the Mollington Banastre
Hotel in Chester and Bulgaria's
players seem singularly unperturbed
by their 2-0 defeat to Brazil the
previous day
Syndication International

Bulgaria's players seem intent on making sure those dour Soviet Bloc stereotypes don't stick
BIPPA Photo Pool

Top The Soviets prepare for their
semi-final with West Germany behind
closed doors at the Lymm Grammar
School gym
Bottom Captain Albert Shesternev
meets supporters outside the Lymm
Hotel vacated by the Brazilians
BIPPA Photo Pool

The Soviet Union and West Germany
sides are piped on to the pitch at
Goodison Park for their semi-final
on 25 July

Andre Lecoq/Robert Legros, L'Equipe

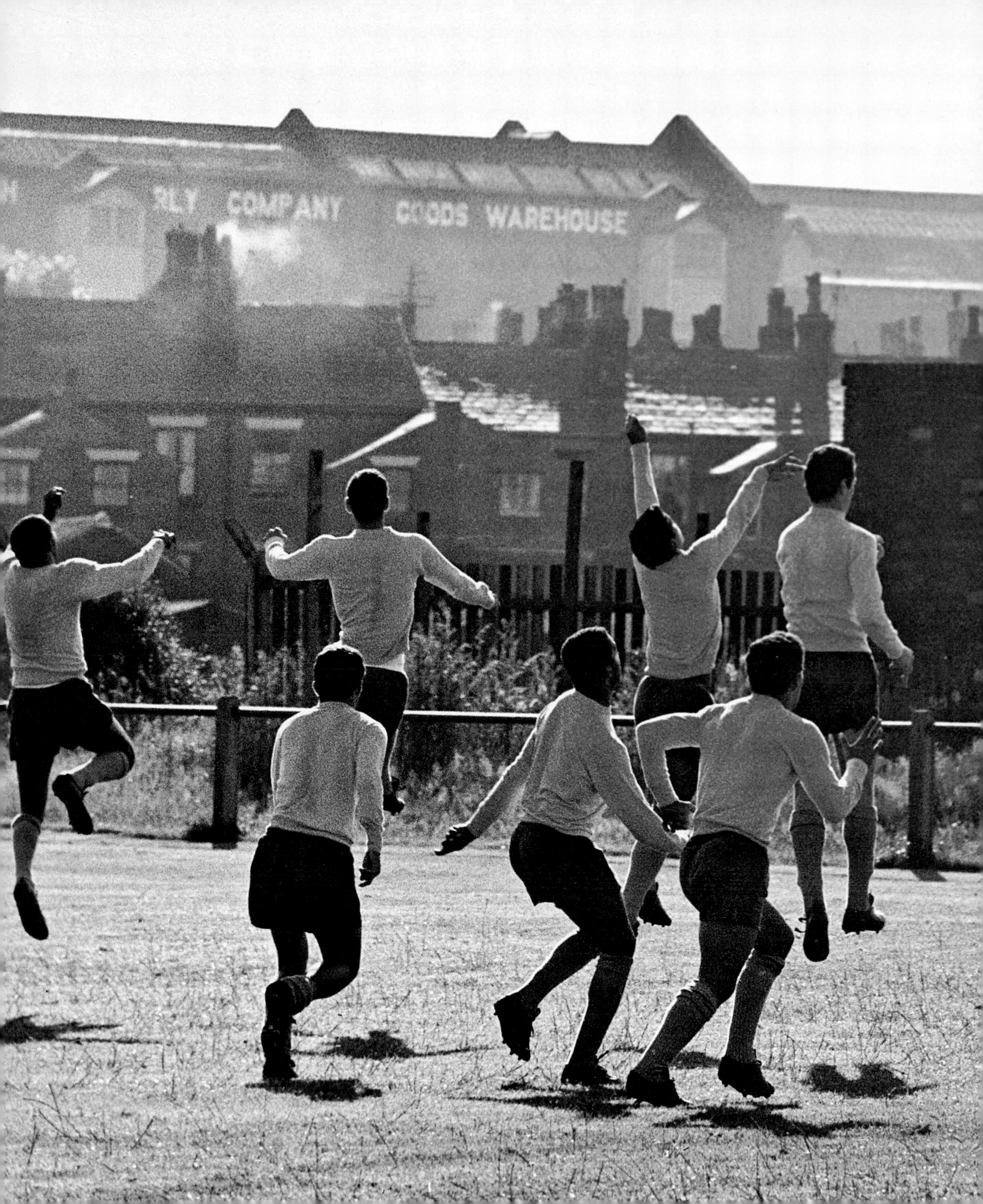
RLY COMPANY GOODS WAREHOUSE

The Brazilians catch some sunlight as they train against the backdrop of industrial Bolton

Pedro De Lima

141

Eusébio leaves Goodison Park on
23 July after his four goals against
North Korea have propelled Portugal
to a place in the semi-finals. He is,
incongruously, drinking from a
hot water bottle, something the
Portugal players did throughout the
tournament, presumably due to
something getting lost in translation
Stephen Shakeshaft, Liverpool Post & Echo

José Torres is fouled and Eusébio
appeals successfully for the penalty
that will enable him to pull the score
against North Korea back to 3-2. St
Luke's church is in the background
Nuno Ferrari, A Bola

Top Hungary goalkeeper Antal Szentmihályi, ruled out of the tournament after being injured in their first game, makes a dive in training
Eric Shaw/George Stephenson, Press Association
Bottom Bulgaria's reserve keeper Simeon Simeonov defends a makeshift goal
BIPPA Photo Pool

Top Portugal's third-choice keeper, Américo Lopes, makes a flying save in training at Southport
Eric Shaw/George Stephenson, Press Association
Bottom Brazil's reserve keeper Manga heads for the mud at Bolton as he prepares to come into the side after the 3-1 defeat against Hungary
BIPPA Photo Pool

Ivan Davidov of Bulgaria (left) finds the Hungarians none too pleased after he has kicked goalkeeper József Gelei in the head. The Bulgarian, making his debut, will later score an own goal equalizer in Hungary's 3-1 win
Peter Sheppard, Mirror

Hungary's Kálmán Mészöly, no doubt prompted by the photographer, reads the front page of the *Mirror*. His team's victory against Brazil is featured on the back
BIPPA Photo Pool

Above Alexandre Baptista of Portugal leapfrogs the postbox in Stanneylands Road, Wilmslow, Cheshire, round the corner from the team hotel
Nuno Ferrari, A Bola
Below High spirits in the camp after the 3-1 defeat of Brazil as José Torres gets a wheelbarrow ride from team-mate Vicente Lucas
BIPPA Photo Pool

SERVICE
PLEASE RING

Goodison echoes to the cry of Hun-gary,
Hun-gary as the
champs fall to ..

MIGHTY MAGYARS!

IN NEXT WEEK'S
DAILY MIRROR

Saints

inners

'Afraid'

Guess who has won..

BEHIND
THE
LINE

.. and who has lost?

WORLD
CUP
MIRROR

PETERS AND PAINE IN ENGLAND TEAM—Page 13

Portugal's Eusébio gives an impromptu pitchside interview at Goodison Park on 23 July after his bravura performance against North Korea in the quarter-final
Eric Shaw/ George Stephenson, Press Association

Flórián Albert (left) and Ferenc Bene of Hungary celebrate their 3-1 victory against Brazil at Goodison Park on 15 July with a drink from a soda syphon. The same picture appears, reversed, on the back of the *Mirror* on page 145
Monte Fresco/Charles Owens, Mirror

János Farkas jumps for joy after scoring Hungary's second goal against Brazil
Monte Fresco/Charles Owens, Mirror

Wrapped in a heavy black coat, Pelé
leaves the Goodison Park pitch with
the beaten Brazil team after their 3-1
defeat to Portugal. Only an unlikely
two-goal win by Bulgaria over
Hungary can see them through now

Express
©Getty Images

After the same game, Eusébio
salutes the crowd who have
witnessed his two goals
Express
©*Getty Images*

Right The much-travelled West Germany fans celebrate semi-final victory against the Soviet Union at Goodison Park on 25 July. Having also visited Hillsborough and Villa Park, they are now bound for Wembley armed with a very professional-looking Uwe Seeler banner
BIPPA Photo Pool

Soviet Union goalkeeper Lev Yashin (right) congratulates his counterpart, West Germany's Hans Tilkowski, on reaching the World Cup final
Press Association

Following page The expressions of the Brazilian staff say it all after the 3-1 defeat to Hungary
Monte Fresco/Charles Owens, Mirror

1966
LONDON

Left The World Cup is on show again to 30 photographers at Cannon Row police station. Holding it is Chief Superintendent William Gilbert. A senior officer said: "It will be kept in a very safe place."
The Guardian

Had the 1966 World Cup run to a slogan, it would surely have been "The Football World Cup – It's Here If You Want It". That's the impression, at least, looking back from our hype-obsessed era. But Britain, it goes without saying, was a different place then, the home of the *Black & White Minstrel Show* and a country where the New Carlton Cabaret Club merrily billed itself as "The gayest night-spot in the Sheffield area". Cinemas were pulling in punters with two X-rated films (both "continental", of course), *Galia* ("Never before has the British censor passed such scenes" – *Daily Express*) and *The Mandrake*, cryptically billed as "Naughty but rude!".

Manchester and Birmingham still had early-closing days and, despite the arrival of the Beatles and Swinging London, the country appeared to be run almost exclusively by a cabal of ex-army officers in blazers and stout brogues. It was the Britain revealed in *Don't Look Back*, D A Pennebaker's documentary on Bob Dylan's 1965 UK tour, a place where even the coolest pop music was presided over by men with handlebar moustaches and regimental ties, the technical side of things in the slightly bewildered hands of a couple of elderly blokes in brown overalls who would attempt to fix just about anything with garden twine and fish-scented glue.

It should be noted that in Britain – the home nations having studiously avoided the tournament until 1950 for fear of what might occur if they came into prolonged contact with foreigners – the *Mundial* wasn't quite the big deal it is now. Indeed, when the newly appointed Minister With Special Responsibility for Sport, Denis Howell, raised the topic with Labour Prime Minister Harold Wilson, he found himself having to explain what the World Cup was.

The wartime generation were not much given to hyperbole and football was still a game. When Wilson eventually understood the nature and importance of the tournament, he allocated £500,000 to fund necessary ground improvements – a sum that was considered so outlandish by senior civil servants some suggested that when the public learned of it they would bring down the government in protest.

So in the circumstances the organizing committee's efforts at promotion were nothing so much as a publicity whirlwind, albeit one whipped up with an eye to costs. Unwilling to spend large amounts on advertising, they dismissed all thought of a TV or newspaper campaign in favour of printing 100,000 posters, which were pasted up in railway stations, airports and social clubs "without a penny being paid for the use of the sites".

Another 30 tons of paper went into the production of ticket brochures, a million of which were printed for distribution in 130 different countries. The FA tried to offset the cost by selling advertising, but such was the general apathy no interested company could be found. Add to this the 250 tons of paper used to produce 1,000,000 copies of the 64-page souvenir programme and it is plain that if the World Cup was good news for printers it was bad news for trees.

The committee did drum up some advertisers for the official guide, though these were not the multinational "partners" of today. Harris's of Perry Barr, for example, could proudly call themselves the "official cleaners for the world cup in the Midlands" and much of the rest of the advertising was taken up by provincial shoe shops, betting offices and coach hire services, giving the guide a pleasantly parochial air that would suffuse the whole tournament. In England in 1966 Pelé, Eusébio and Mazzola lined up with Saxon's (Of Sunderland), Mowbray Motors and the Belle Vue Zoo Park.

The official insignia had been unveiled in early 1965. Designed by Arthur Bew, a commercial artist who had lost a leg during World War II, it featured the Jules Rimet trophy, the FA coat of arms and a football

The president meets the prime minister. Stanley Rous (left) of Fifa and Harold Wilson at a press conference on 8 July, three days before the start of the tournament
Evening Standard
©Getty Images

"globe", all superimposed on a Union Flag (Britain and England were still synonymous – at least to the English). The design had the gravitas for which the committee was searching, but they quickly recognized that it was not the sort of thing that had a more general commercial application, particularly for merchandising. For that they needed something a bit different, which was where World Cup Willie came in.

The little lion was designed by Reg Hoye and launched in July 1965. The name had originally been applied by female staff to the organization's chief administrative officer, E K Willson. Oddly enough, Mr Willson was also short and square-shouldered, though he had somewhat less hair than his cartoon namesake and apparently didn't favour the Union Jack waistcoat. Willie proved hugely popular. He had a hit single and his own special World Cup ale, and his image appeared on a bewildering range of products, including dartboards, periscopes, cigars and horse brasses. Royalties netted the organizers around five per cent on all items sold.

Despite these efforts and a successful range of World Cup stamps, the biggest publicity coup had nothing to do with the committee. After some debate it had been

England's squad get wet on 9 June, as the fountain is turned on while they are relaxing at the Lilleshall recreation centre in Shropshire
George Phillips, Sun
© Mirrorpix

agreed that the Jules Rimet trophy should be displayed, under strictest security, on the Stanley Gibbons stand at the Stampex Exhibition at Central Hall, Westminster. On the morning of Sunday 20 March it was found to have been stolen. The theft made headlines round the world. As the official FA report, not without a little glow of pride, commented: "An atomic explosion could scarcely have been given more coverage."

The police launched a feverish investigation. Joe Mears, the FA chairman, an elderly man with a pale moustache, round spectacles and the look of the sort of uncle who would know his way around a fret saw, received phone calls purportedly from the thieves demanding a ransom. A typed note was so full of threats about melting pots and sudden bursts of capital letters that it could be the inspiration for Dr Evil in the Austin Powers films. A few days later the trophy's removable top arrived in the post and Scotland Yard pounced on a suspect, Edward Bletchley. He was later sentenced to two years in prison. The cup, though, was nowhere to be found.

A week after it had first been reported missing, in a piece of scripting straight from an Ealing comedy, the trophy was recovered in a garden in Beulah Hill,

south London, not by the police (still bobbies in those days, still blowing whistles, wearing capes and cuffing errant youngsters round the ear, and not a man among them under 50) but by a mongrel dog named Pickles. Pickles went on to gain some fame (his owner was the somewhat less well-known David Corbett). He appeared on TV and in a feature film alongside Eric Sykes before dying tragically, strangled to death while chasing a cat. The Jules Rimet trophy, meanwhile, retired from the limelight to recover from its ordeal. It did not appear in public again until the Queen handed it over to Bobby Moore on 30 July.

Ticketing was a major worry. Knowing what was available, at what price and where took considerable organization. The ticket control room managed it, though, with a state-of-the-art arrangement of specially marked blackboards and lots of packets of coloured chalk. To thwart the forgers, the committee commissioned the manufacture of five tons of watermarked paper to make the 2,094,435 tickets that would go on sale. Season tickets for the best seats at the final, third-place match, one semi-final, one quarter-final and six group matches were sold for £25 and 15 shillings. A standing season ticket for the same games came in at £3, seven shillings and sixpence. Such was the success of the publicity campaign that by the end of 1965 tickets worth more than £500,000 had been sold, more than a third of them overseas.

In the previous World Cup, in Chile in 1962, there had been a minor crisis when it emerged that there weren't sufficient match balls in the country. So tenders were invited and 111 different balls from nine manufacturers were scrutinized by Fifa at the Olympic Restaurant at White City stadium. After careful testing that included measuring, weighing and bouncing the balls on hard and soft surfaces, the footballs offered by Slazenger were chosen

and an order for 400 balls in shades lemon, orange and white were placed.

The opening ceremony on 11 July was, by current standards, a modest affair. "Simple, yet colourful" was the brief for the organizers. To this end they bussed in schoolboys from Hendon, Willesden, Finchley and Hammersmith, dressed them in the strips of the 16 competing countries and got them to march round the pitch to the music of the massed bands of the Coldstream and Irish Guards. The grand finale came when the 16 flags were unfurled simultaneously from 25-foot steel flagpoles around Wembley's roof. "There was an audible crack as the flags billowed out, sufficient to draw a gasp of astonishment from the packed arena," an FA observer would recall. Wooden lolly sticks that had been stuck into the lanyards of the flagpoles by chief engineer George Stanton supplied the audible crack. Then out came England and Uruguay to start the real business.

The England players appeared understandably nervous. Along with Brazil they were favourites to win, but unlike the South Americans the nation had no World Cup pedigree whatsoever. Their position owed something to home advantage, a bit to the quality of their players and a little more to the style and manner of the team's manager, Alf Ramsey. Ramsey belonged to a wartime generation of men whose inner workings were mysterious, you suspect even to themselves. He seemed uncomfortable in his own skin and certainly uncomfortable with his background. Asked about where his parents lived he replied: "Dagenham, I believe." He took elocution lessons and, in public at least, spoke as if terrified that industrial language would slip out if he didn't keep a careful grip on it.

Yet despite an apparent unbending attitude to all things, particularly discipline, there was an absurdist streak to him worthy of fellow east Londoner Max Wall. When

England players broke curfew, they might come back to find that Alf had unmade their beds, or simply placed their passports on their pillows. Elliptical though they were, these punishments seem to have had the desired effect. One man who received the latter treatment was Jimmy Greaves. "We interpreted it to mean that if we misbehaved again we would not travel abroad with the England team," he said.

Alf's combination of the stern and the bizarre kept players on their toes. More than that, his steely determination shone through. He had announced in 1964 that England would win the World Cup and one look at his piercing, dark eyes told you that this was not a man to argue with.

Ramsey had attempted to keep the England players relaxed. They had spent a lot of time playing cricket, Jimmy Greaves showing an unexpected talent as an off-spinner. They had also paid a visit to Pinewood Studios, where Sean Connery was filming the new James Bond film, *You Only Live Twice*. In their natty suits the England players didn't look out of place. Greaves, in fact, appeared a natural replacement should the Scotsman ever relinquish the role. The players got to talk racehorses with Yul Brynner, while Norman Wisdom was on hand so none of the squad had to do an impression of him. At the end of the visit Ramsey gave a speech of thanks making special mention of Connery, whose name he repeatedly mispronounced as "Seen".

There was not much comedy in the opening game, intentional or otherwise. England's opponents, Uruguay, showed no ambition other than to secure a point. They played Horacio Troche as a sweeper and withdrew their two most creative players, Pedro Rocha and Julio Cortés, deep into midfield. At the first sign of England breaching this defensive line they produced a body check or an over-the-top tackle. Even the formidable Nobby

Stiles took a kicking. England won 16 corners, but Uruguay's excellent goalkeeper, Ladislao Mazurkiewicz, nicknamed "the Grey Ghost", was hardly bothered all afternoon. The most noteworthy thing about the match was that Uruguay coach Ondino Viera picked his son Milton – the only time this happened in a World Cup finals before 1998. At the final whistle the Uruguayans danced about in delight to a chorus of derision from the stands.

France had thrashed England in Ramsey's first game in charge, but since then had been sliding gradually downhill. Like the France teams of recent vintage they were noted for their speed, but unlike the sides that won the World Cup in 1998 and the European Championship in 2000 their

defence was suspect. Mexico were regarded as also-rans. Their previous appearance at Wembley had seen them hammered 8-0, yet they gave France no end of trouble, opening the scoring when their best forward, the tall and elegant Enrique Borja, netted from close range. France's vaunted midfield playmaker, the Argentina-born Néstor Combin (who played for Juventus), was anonymous, but *Les Bleus* eventually found an equalizer when Gérard Hausser's low shot from 20 yards went in off the post.

France's next game against Uruguay was played at White City in pouring rain. The old stadium was the home of the organizing committee and the venue's only game was partly a present for the staff and partly the result of Wembley having been pre-booked

Jacky Simon needs help to leave the Wembley pitch at the end of the game after being badly fouled by Nobby Stiles during England's 2-0 victory against France on 20 July
Andre Lecoq/ Robert Legros, L'Equipe

Mexico fans
celebrate in style
after the 1-1 draw
with France at
Wembley on 13 July,
perhaps to the
bemusement of
goalkeeper Ignacio
Calderón and the
No 15, Guillermo
Hernández

Terry Fincher, Express
©Getty Images

for greyhound racing. The weather that afternoon was awful, with constant rain and the sky so dark that the floodlights had to be switched on before kick-off. France replaced the ineffectual Combin with the lively Jacques Simon, whose busy, neat style provided good service to the forwards, Hausser and Yves Herbet. Uruguay had snuffed out England's attacking threat easily, but much to the displeasure of the watching Ramsey they struggled to contain the French. Herbet burst into the penalty area, was tripped by Jorge Manicera and Hector de Bourcoing (another Argentine, who had played for his native country back in the mid-1950s) slotted home the penalty.

Surprisingly, Uruguay burst into life and scored twice through the upright Rocha and the speedy Cortés. Lead secured, they reverted to the defensive measures they had employed at Wembley. Hausser hit the crossbar, but apart from that France foundered. Frustrated, Simon gobbed on Dr Karol Galba, the Czech referee, who, in keeping with the *laissez-faire* standards of the tournament, only booked him.

For the game against Mexico, Ramsey dropped John Connelly and Alan Ball and brought in sturdy Southampton winger Terry Paine and Martin Peters of West Ham.

Ramsey famously described Peters as "10 years ahead of his time". His team-mates were less gnomic. They called him the Duke of Kent because of his gaunt, patrician profile. Peters was a decent header of the ball, a good passer, but most of all he did rather nebulous things incredibly well. Creating space, ghosting, doing his best work off the ball, this was the stuff Peters was good at. He was such a master of subtlety he seemed to be almost invisible.

After their lively display against France, the Mexicans appeared a spent force. "On the evidence of this performance Mexico have as much right to be in the World Cup as the Isle of Man has to be represented on the UN Security Council," thundered Hugh McIlvanney in the *Observer*. Certainly they lacked ambition. At kick-off, Isidoro Díaz hammered the ball up the field and his team-mates back-tracked towards their own penalty area. The England fans chanted: "We want goals, we want goals." Eventually they got them. Bobby Charlton, a player whose brilliance was constantly undermined by his lugubrious manner and unfortunate hairstyle, featured heavily in both.

The younger Charlton brother could pass long or short, or dribble at deceptive pace, employing a cunning bodyswerve, and shoot with thunderous power and accuracy with both feet. Now he took possession and sprinted forward, dodged from one foot to the other, sending defenders scattering, and finally hammered the ball with such force it seems to change shape in mid-air as it whooshed into the net. For the second he exchanged passes over on the left before threading the ball through to Greaves. His shot was parried by Ignacio Calderón and fell to Hunt, who side-footed home in an immaculate style that recalled the drawings in the "how to pass" section of a teach-yourself-soccer manual. It was a frustrating and patchy game, but England had won. The crowd sung so enthusiastically that the singularly unimpressed McIlvanney

speculated that Fifa might want to start dope-testing spectators.

Mexico needed to beat Uruguay by two goals to qualify. Given that the South Americans only needed a point to go through, this seemed highly unlikely, a fact the coach Ignacio Trelles seemed to acknowledge by bringing in the veteran goalkeeper Antonio Carbajal. Carbajal was 37 and had made his World Cup debut in Brazil in 1950. He thus became the longest-serving player in the competition's history, and is still one of only two to play in five tournaments (the other being Germany's Lothar Matthäus). Mexico, spurred on by the English crowd's enthusiastic chanting of "Me-hikko... Me-hikko", played better than anyone expected and so did Uruguay. But the game ended 0-0. The Wembley audience seemed to be getting the message about what was on offer: although the official attendance is given as 61,112, actually only about 35,000 turned up.

France had struggled in every other match but roused themselves for the game with England, which they needed to win by two clear goals to progress. They attacked predominantly through the middle, using the speed of Philippe Gondet to turn Jack Charlton and Moore, while at the back their offside trap constantly caught Hunt and Greaves. Banks was brought into action, as he had been all tournament. England's frustration began to show. The press had dubbed the dentally challenged Nobby Stiles "the toothless tiger", but if he didn't have teeth he did have studs. Fed up with proceedings, the midfielder took out Jacky Simon with a tackle he later admitted was "bad, bad". The referee, Peru's Arturo Yamasaki, was sufficiently vexed by it to book Stiles and Fifa were apparently so shocked by the recklessness of the lunge that they demanded he be suspended by the English FA. Ramsey stood by his man, though, and eventually the matter was dropped. On the field Hunt again side-footed in a rebound, this time after Jack Charlton's header had come back off the post, and later looked on as French keeper Marcel Aubour made a hash of his header from Ian Callaghan's cross, pushing it into the net instead of round the post.

As the game petered out Jimmy Greaves suffered a gash to the leg that would keep him out of the quarter-finals. He had had a poor time of it, anyway. Later he would blame his problems on the fact that he was recovering from hepatitis, the same pernicious virus that would later cause Gary Lineker to blast so many chances over the bar in the 1988 European Championship.

Ramsey had been keeping an eye on England's next opponents, Argentina, and had clearly made up his mind about them. "Well, gentlemen," he said, "you know the kind of game you have on your hands this afternoon." Geoff Hurst replaced the injured Greaves and Alan Ball was brought back on the right side of midfield for his combative qualities.

It was a sunny afternoon and the shadows of the players lay across Wembley as ominous and dramatic as anything in *Citizen Kane*. Ironically the villain of the piece, Antonio Rattín, was a devout Anglophile who firmly believed that if his nation had been a British colony it would have ended up like Australia or Canada and been an altogether happier place.

German referee Rudolf Kreitlein was small with a bald pate and hair that sprouted wildly around his ears, giving him the appearance of Professor Branestawm. Rattín, by contrast, was tall and lean. The huge muscles on his thighs twitched and his face switched from anguish to bewilderment without ever quite shaking off an overall impression of disdain. With his unruly dark quiff, he looked like a gang leader from *West Side Story*.

From kick-off, Rattín loomed over the diminutive Kreitlein at every opportunity. In the canine world, this sort of behaviour invariable ends in a fight. It was no different now. Kreitlein got crosser and crosser and noted more and more names down in his book ("One was reminded," wrote Brian Glanville in the *Sunday Times*, "of a schoolboy collecting engine numbers"). In the end, Rattín, who had already been booked – a decision he greeted by spitting at the referee's feet – towered once too often. Like a terrier Kreitlein cracked, though instead of biting his adversary the little German dismissed him with an angry flutter of his left hand after he disputed a free-kick awarded against Alberto González.

Rattín refused to leave. He is reputed to be a millionaire, the owner of a vast cork forest, and now displayed the weary arrogance of a man of means. His team-mates surrounded the referee. Eight long minutes passed. The crowd began to slow handclap and chanted: "Oh why are we waiting?" Ken Aston, responsible for referees' logistics at the tournament, came on to the field to try to sort things out. "It became plain to me that if no solution could be found the game would have to be abandoned and awarded to England. That would have been catastrophic," he would recall. Aston had presided over the "Battle of Santiago" between Italy and Chile in 1962 – a game he couldn't control even with the aid of his famous "Acme Thunderer" whistle – but now he calmly and patiently led Rattín away. Convinced that the Argentine really had failed to understand that he had been sent off, Aston would later successfully campaign for the introduction of red and yellow cards. The England players either looked baffled, or, in the case of Martin Peters at least, highly amused. Cor, foreigners, eh?

Kreitlein later explained that the Argentina captain had been dismissed for what he described as "violence of the tongue". Later he revised this to "the look on his face". Rattín protested that all he was doing was appealing for an interpreter.

The game had been violent from the start, filled with bodychecks, trips, hacks, nips, pokes, hair-pulling and spitting. Even the normally saintly Bobby Charlton was moved to seek retribution (though, as his team-mate Alan Ball once noted: "Everyone

**Goalkeeper Ladislao
Mazurkiewicz
celebrates after
helping Uruguay to
a goalless draw
against England in
the opening match
of the tournament,
at Wembley on
11 July**
Tony Harris/
Mark Seymour,
Press Association

has Bobby marked down as soft, but a player of his skill doesn't survive as long as he did unless he can look after himself") and got booked for his trouble. After the sending-off things deteriorated still further. Amid the brutality Hurst stole in to head home a cross from the mysterious Peters, the game's only goal. A small boy ran on to the field to celebrate and was belted round the head by the indignant Oscar Más.

The aftermath saw Alf stopping George Cohen from swapping his shirt and branding his opponents "animals" (a comment for which he received a warning from the disciplinary committee). There were many allegations of bad behaviour: an orange spat in the face of a Fifa official, a substitute urinating on the threshold of the England dressing room, their bus kicked and beaten. Bobby Charlton observed: "It was a sordid business." Nobby Stiles was more sanguine: "Apart from the violence, I came through with no problems."

Was Rattín's sending-off justified? The charge of "foul or abusive language", grounds for a straight dismissal, certainly founders on the fact that Rattín could speak no German while Herr Kreitlein spoke no Spanish. On the other hand, he had already been booked and a second caution could

easily have been for dissent "by word or action" – the Argentine's attitude needed little interpretation. Rattín clearly thought it was an injustice, suspecting that darker forces were at work at Wembley. "England was the last World Cup before satellite television. In all the World Cups from '66 back the host nation always won or was a finalist [Not actually true unless France in 1938, Switzerland in 1954 or Chile in 1962 somehow sneaked in without anybody noticing] because Fifa was always sweating that if the host nation didn't do well the tournament would be a failure."

England captain Bobby Moore was calm and assured. He didn't chase opponents, but waited until they came to him. With his blond hair and phlegmatic approach, he seemed to epitomize the qualities of British legend. According to Moore, semi-final opponents Portugal were the West Ham of international football, exciting to watch, cultured, but ultimately too vulnerable to survive. Too nice as well, perhaps. They had dropped the vicious João Morais and failed to man-mark England's dangerman Bobby Charlton. Ramsey, in contrast, allocated Nobby Stiles to do a job on Eusébio. For once the Manchester United midfielder didn't produce much rough stuff (the game was remarkably clean, without so much as a foul until the 23rd minute), but his presence and England's habit of backing off rather than diving into tackles helped nullify the threat of the "Black Panther". Bobby Charlton, meanwhile, floated free across the Wembley turf. He scored after good work by Hunt who, belying his reputation as wholesome yet stodgy, the footballing equivalent of porridge, neatly beat José Carlos and bore down on José Pereira, who opted to tackle with his feet rather than use his hands. The sliding challenge knocked the ball into the path of Charlton, who side-footed into the net. His second was a classic, one of the most famous scored at Wembley. Hurst recovered Cohen's long

ball on the byeline, shuffled past Carlos and rolled the ball back to the No 9. His shot was hit low but with such power that it seemed to lift off midway through its flight into the net.

It wasn't all over. Mário Coluna had an excellent game in midfield and the massive José Torres was too big even for Jack Charlton to knock over. Portugal received a penalty when the elder Charlton handled Torres's goalbound header and Eusébio scored. Banks saved brilliantly from Coluna and soon afterwards advanced rapidly to force António Simões to shoot wide. It was the last significant action of the match.

An entertaining game and, perhaps more importantly given what had gone before, a clean and sporting one. "This performance rammed the words of censure down the ranting throats of the defeated and envious teams of South America," snarled an unforgiving Desmond Hackett in the *Daily Express*, who, you sensed, wouldn't have let Rattín off the field without a couple of fourpenny ones.

With England through to the final, World Cup fever at last gripped the nation. Or so it seems, for what other explanation could there be for around 70,000 turning up to watch the third-place play-off, a game that is apparently designed as an anti-climax?

Both teams played like losers. Eusébio scored from the spot again – his ninth goal of the competition – this time after Murtaz Khurtsilava had handled, partly in panic at the sheer stature of Torres. The Soviet Union equalized when the latest goalkeeping error let in Eduard Malofeyev. In the 88th minute, Torres rose yet again, his knockback fell to José Augusto, who chipped it straight back to him and the big man guided the ball gently past Lev Yashin. At the final whistle the famous Russian keeper walked off with a wave and a flash of nicotine-stained teeth. He was old now. Eusébio was not, yet surprisingly it was the last World Cup appearance for both the Black Panther and the Black Octopus.

London schoolboys rehearse their roles in the opening ceremony at Wembley Stadium on 8 July 1966, three days before the real thing
BIPPA Photo Pool

A souvenir seller with a full array of
rosettes and pennants at Wembley on
11 July, ahead of the opening game
Pedro De Lima

Following page Fans arrive at
Wembley for the opening game. But
for the rosettes on the two men at the
far left there's little evidence of a big
match. In the background are the
Wembley stadium offices, in the
foreground a dispatch rider's bike
ready to pick up photographers' films
for development
Charlie Ley/Eric Piper, Mirror

The West German mascots march out at Wembley for the opening ceremony on 11 July – the team themselves will put in an appearance at the stadium for the final on 30 July

Andre Lecoq/Robert Legros, L'Equipe

The Queen is suitably impressed at
the opening ceremony by a model of
some cattle, a gift to her from the
Uruguayan FA
Monte Fresco, Mirror

Jimmy Greaves offers some
heading advice to comedian
Norman Wisdom when England
visit Pinewood Studios on 12 July
Derek Millward, Press Association

Antonio Rattín, the anglophile captain
of Argentina, goes sightseeing in
London on 25 July, two days after
his infamous dismissal in the
quarter-final against England. He had
harsh words for the competition's
organizers: "All I can say is that
England will win the World Cup –
because the referees are on their side."
Syndication International

Bobby Moore leads out his England side before their quarter-final with Argentina at Wembley on 23 July
Original source unknown

Roberto Sosa and Héctor Salva of Uruguay arrive at Wembley for the opening match on 11 July. Neither of them got a game, though Salva played against West Germany in the quarter-final at Hillsborough
Andre Lecoq/Robert Legros, L'Equipe

Antonio Rattín argues with officials after referee Rudolf Kreitlein has sent him off in the quarter-final against England at Wembley on 23 July. "I was sent off because I asked for one minute with an interpreter because the referee couldn't understand me," he claimed. Kreitlein later forlornly reflected: "I have no intention of bringing charges against the Argentinian players. I just want to forget the match."

Monte Fresco, Mirror

Trainer Les Cocker hands an exhausted
Bobby Charlton an orange at the end
of the acrimonious quarter-final. Some
shirts have been swapped, despite Alf
Ramsey famously preventing George
Cohen from doing so

Tony Harris/Mark Seymour,
Press Association

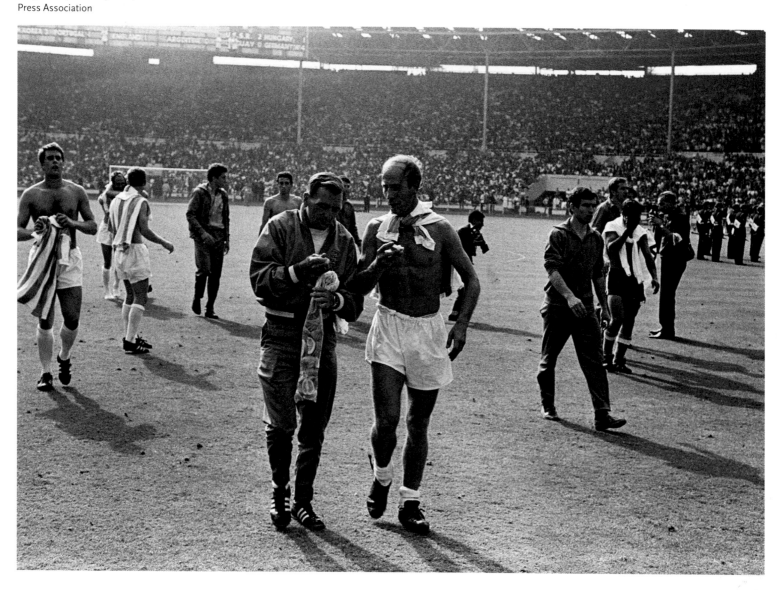

Linda Clarke, an 18-year-old office worker, shows off Watney's commemorative pale ale, in a glass complete with World Cup Willie

The archetypal World Cup family, surrounded by practically every commodity that could be bought for the event
Original source unknown

Bobby Moore takes a seat on the England bus, with Jimmy Greaves a couple of steps ahead
Andre Lecoq/Robert Legros, L'Equipe

Trainer Les Cocker, manager Alf
Ramsey, physio Harold Shepherdson
and Jimmy Greaves read the papers
during a training session at
Roehampton on 15 July

Press Association

Uruguay take lunch at the Brent Bridge hotel on the way to White City for the game against France
BIPPA Photo Pool

Jimmy Greaves finishes his breakfast at Hendon Hall Hotel on 9 July and reads the Saturday *Sportsmail*, two days before the opening game
Wally Lockyear, Press Association

Enrique Borja (No 20) is embraced by ecstatic team-mates after giving Mexico the lead against France in the 1-1 draw at Wembley on 13 July
BIPPA Photo Pool

Nobby Stiles resorts to an overhead
kick under pressure from Robert
Budzinski of France in England's 2-0
win at Wembley on 20 July
BIPPA Photo Pool

England reserve goalkeeper Ron
Springett leads Nobby Stiles out of
a record shop in Golders Green on
27 July, the day after the semi-final
victory over Portugal
Nick Beer, Press Association

An eager young fan chases England's
Bobby Moore (left) and Martin Peters
as they take a morning stroll near the
team's hotel in Hendon on 23 July, the
day of the quarter-final with Argentina
BIPPA Photo Pool

Members of the Uruguay squad
watch closely as the goalposts are
dismantled (in order for the pitch to
be marked out) after their 20-minute
training session on the Wembley turf
on 7 July
George Stephenson, Press Association

Mexico's José Luis González takes
a long slurp from the water-bag held
by trainer Francisco Larios during a
break from exercise at Cheshunt in
Hertfordshire on 5 July
Mark Seymour, Press Association

France's Laurent Robuschi watches as
team-mate Gérard Hausser samples
English coiffure
BIPPA Photo Pool

Bobby Charlton (No 9) watches as his shot flies into the net for England's opening goal during the 2-0 win against Mexico at Wembley on 16 July. Looking on are, from left, Jesús Del Muro (hiding goalkeeper Ignacio Calderón), Ignacio Jáuregui, Roger Hunt, Gustavo Peña and Gabriel Núñez

Tony Harris/Mark Seymour, Press Association

Geoff Hurst, cheeks puffed, fires a shot at goal during the 1-0 win in the quarter-final with Argentina at Wembley on 23 July
Tony Harris/Mark Seymour,
Press Association

**Ignacio Calderón, the Mexico
goalkeeper, says a prayer before the
England game on 16 July**
Syndication International

**Bobby Charlton takes a stroll by
himself in Hendon on 23 July, the day
of the Argentina game**
BIPPA Photo Pool

Following page Julio César Cortés
celebrates scoring the winning goal in
Uruguay's 2-1 victory against France
at White City on 15 July
Norman Quicke, Express
©Getty Images

193

**Jimmy Greaves enjoys a glass of beer
at the same function**
Derek Millward, Press Association

**Bobby and Jack Charlton afford
themselves a broad grin along with a
pint and a cigarette. They are
christening England's World Cup suits
at the Anglo-American Sporting Club
dinner at a London hotel on 21 June**
Derek Millward, Press Association

Eusébio acknowledges the applause
of the crowd for the last time in a
World Cup finals as he leaves
Wembley after the 2-1 win over the
Soviet Union in the third-place
play-off on 28 July, having scored his
ninth goal of the tournament
George Phillips, Sun
©Mirrorpix

Eusébio at the Sporting Club in
Knightsbridge on 31 July, feeling flush
after picking up his cheque for £1000
for finishing as top scorer
Clive Limpkin, Express
©Getty Images

Geoff Hurst runs in front of the row of photographers after heading the only goal of the quarter-final against Argentina at Wembley on 23 July. The picture is one of a set of three that are seen as classic images despite the fact that the face of the subject is, unconventionally for sports photography, out of shot
BIPPA Photo Pool

Portugal succumb at last to England
in the semi-final at Wembley on
26 July. Eusébio wipes away his tears
Gerry Cranham

England players celebrate reaching the final after their 2-1 win against Portugal
BIPPA Photo Pool

Following page **England reserve goalkeeper Ron Springett and Jimmy Greaves take a drink with James Bond, in the shape of Sean Connery, at Pinewood Studios on 12 July**
Mirrorpix

1966 FINAL

Wembley, 30 July. Bobby Moore lifts the Jules Rimet trophy above the heads of the crowd around the royal box, with (for 1966) a rare Cross of St George fluttering

Monte Fresco/ Kent Gavin, Mirror

Warnings about forged tickets for the final abounded, but there seemed little to fear. Guarding Wembley on 30 July was commissionaire Tom Sawyer, a 74-year-old with stern eyebrows and, it would turn out later, a vague resemblance to the eagle newsreader from *The Muppet Show*. Tom was constantly on the lookout for scams. "I can spot a shyster a mile off," he commented in a manner that brooked no argument.

In Coventry Street a sign in a shop window showed a bulldog standing triumphantly on a daschund beneath the caption "Roll On Saturday", but generally patriotism was less bellicose than today: there was no singing of the *Dam Busters* theme at Wembley. Indeed there would be little singing at all once the match kicked off, though the chant of "England!" was given some rhythmic punch by a Brazilian drummer who had bought a ticket for the final in the hope of seeing Pelé.

Jimmy Greaves was fit again, but despite the rumours it never seemed likely that Alf Ramsey would bring him back. Geoff Hurst had come in and scored in the quarter-final then set up Bobby Charlton's second in the semi. Greaves had an impressive overall record for England, but in seven World Cup matches he had scored only once.

Having watched Charlton's magisterial display against Portugal, West Germany coach Helmut Schön decide to man-mark him. Oddly, he decided the player for the job was his most creative midfield force, Franz Beckenbauer. Beckenbauer snuffed Charlton out all right, but in so doing he snuffed himself out, too. It was an odd lapse from the wily Schön, who might have done better bringing in the limpet-like Klaus-Dieter Sieloff and allowing the man who would be the Kaiser to wander.

The pitch was slippery after rain and it seemed to suit the Germans. In the 13th minute Sigi Held struck a speculative cross from the left. Gordon Banks shouted to Ray Wilson to leave it, but the full-back mistook his call for a warning and went up too early, and his poor header fell for Helmut Haller in a good position. The forward's shot was weak, but it somehow evaded Jack Charlton and Banks, both of whom appeared to think that the other would deal with it.

Irritated by the sloppy goal, Bobby Moore advanced further forward than normal six minutes later and was brought down. Without waiting for the referee's whistle he clipped the free-kick into the box and right on to the head of the on-rushing Hurst. In the German goal Hans Tilkowski stood and watched the West Ham man's downward header fly into the goal like somebody glancing at a passing car.

An hour of stalemate passed, until Alan Ball's corner from the right found Hurst. His optimistic shot was blocked by Horst-Dieter Höttges. The rebound fell to Martin Peters, who drove it in from seven yards despite the close attentions of Big Jack, who himself seemed to be shaping to shoot. Seeing the ball hit the back of the net, Bobby Charlton ran towards Nobby Stiles, yelling: "We've won it! We've won it! They can't beat us now!" Nobby laughed happily in response. There were only 12 minutes left. Ramsey's team had the best defence in the tournament. It appeared done and dusted.

But with a minute to go, the Swiss referee Gottfried Dienst awarded a free-kick against Jack Charlton for leaning on Held, though the Leeds man made the motion to show that he felt the German had "made a back for him". Lothar Emmerich blasted the free-kick and it pinballed around the penalty area. Moore appealed for hands against Karl-Heinz Schnellinger – not given – and somehow the ball ended up with Wolfgang Weber, who banged it over the desperately lunging Wilson (full first name Ramon, thanks to his mother's fondness for Hollywood star Ramon Navarro) and past Banks. The final would go into extra time

for the first time since 1934, when Italy beat Czechoslovakia 2-1 in Rome.

At the final whistle Ramsey earned his money. Painfully tight-lipped normally, he delivered a rousing admonition: "You've won it once, now go out and win it again." While the West Germans collapsed on the turf England, at Alf's insistence, stood, to show their strength. A psychological ploy in the days before mind games even existed.

In extra time, Ball was out on his feet but somehow managed to outrun Schnellinger and fasten on to Stiles' long ball. From out by the right corner flag he fired in a cross. Hurst evaded his marker, Willi Schulz, controlled the centre and crashed a mighty shot off the underside of the bar. As it bounced down Hunt wheeled away with arm aloft, claiming a goal. Some would point to this as a sign that the ball must have crossed the line, as Hunt would have followed in if it hadn't. The Liverpool man admits, however, that he only did it because he knew he wouldn't have got to the ball anyway, which rather blows that theory out of the water. Instead, Weber headed it over the bar and prepared for a corner. But the referee went across to his linesman, Tofik Bakhramov. Though usually referred to as Russian, Bakhramov was actually from

Members of the England squad take a meal on 29 July, the day before the final. Geoff Hurst glances ruefully over the shoulder of Jimmy Greaves, whose place he took in the team

Terry Fincher, Express
©Getty Images

Uwe Seeler is the crestfallen player. To West Germany this picture came to symbolize the team's unlucky defeat in the final. In 2003 it was voted the greatest football picture ever by the VDS, the German sportswriters' association
Sven Simon

Azerbaijan: the national stadium in Baku is named after him. The linesman from what was then part of the Soviet Union told Dienst that the ball had crossed the line.

A year later the FA were adamant that the "the probing motion-picture cameras" used by the makers of *Goal!*, the official film of the series, "established unquestionably the validity of the goal". But they would say that, wouldn't they?

The West Germans wilted. With a minute left Moore, characteristically cool, chested the ball down in his own penalty area and, with everyone screaming for him to hoof the ball out of the ground, hit a raking pass upfield for Hurst. His West Ham buddy carried the ball forward and hit a shot with such force he took off into the

air himself. Up on the gantries, ITV's Hugh Johns followed the action: "Here's Hurst, he might make it three. He has! He has!... So that's it. That is it!" Sadly for the likable Johns, his words were not to go down in history. He, like Greaves, would be an absence rather than a presence in the story.

For most of us that will remain the image of the World Cup: Hurst, hovering above the pitted Wembley turf, his cheeks puffed out with effort, left leg extended, left arm swinging out, a Cossack dancer in mid leap. Thirty-two years later he would be knighted for his efforts, proof of how the importance of the day mushroomed in the vacuum that has followed since.

At the final whistle, Big Jack knelt with his head in his hands, brother Bobby wept

buckets, Ball turned cartwheels and Stiles leapt on Cohen's back, much to the full-back's embarrassment ("It looked like copulation. I don't know what he was doing, but I didn't enjoy it very much," he later said). Ramsey, meanwhile, sat impassive on the bench even as the crowd chanted his name.

Later, after the official reception at the Royal Garden Hotel in Kensington, while Big Jack and the boys were making an impromptu tour of pubs amid what was described as London's biggest celebration since VE night, Ramsey returned to Wembley and, in the empty, silent, floodlit stadium, ran a solo lap of honour. The following day the hotel had to call in the builders to replace stonework that had been chipped away by souvenir hunters. Though perhaps the hoteliers were lucky. Had the fans known the iconic status this singular result would come to take on for English football, they might have dismantled and carried away the whole place.

The World Cup had been a huge success. It was watched by more fans than any previous tournament and posted record profits. The total gate receipts for the tournament were £1,551,099 13s 6d. The 12,000,000 4d stamps specially issued by the Post Office with the words "England Winners" overprinted on them were sold out by lunchtime of the day they went on sale. Everybody involved made money.

Well, almost everybody. Amazingly, the merchandising was not a success. Eighteen weeks after the final, in a warehouse in the East End of London among boxes filled with ladies' jumpers, marshmallows, birdseed and cat food, auctioneer Philip Silverstone sold off the assets of the bankrupt World Cup Collectors' Club. World Cup Willie drums, bath mats and braces all went under the hammer. An antique dealer, Ron Jones, picked up 22 World Cup flags for £5 10s. He used the Brazilian flag as a cloth on his sideboard.

Cissie Charlton,
in London to see her
boys play, is greeted
by station staff at
King's Cross station
the day before the
final
Jimmy Gray, Keystone

Ushered in by police on a white horse,
the West Germany coach receives a
warm reception on arrival at Wembley
Andre Lecoq/Robert Legros, L'Equipe

The West Germany players head for
Hyde Park during a sight-seeing trip in
London on 27 July. Left to right are
Bernd Patzke, Horst Höttges, Sepp
Maier, Günter Bernard, Werner
Krämer and Friedel Lutz
BIPPA Photo Pool

An England rosette among the scattering of Union Flags as the atmosphere builds at Wembley
Neil Leifer

The West Germans arrive at their hotel in Welwyn Garden City to prepare for the final on 26 July and Lothar Emmerich is happy to sign autographs
BIPPA Photo Pool

A fan dressed as a chimney sweep (a symbol of good luck in Germany) is congratulated on his prediction for the World Cup final scoreline by squad adviser Bert Trautmann (left) and chief press officer "Doctor" Wilfried Gerhardt on the morning of the game
Dennis Evans, Press Association

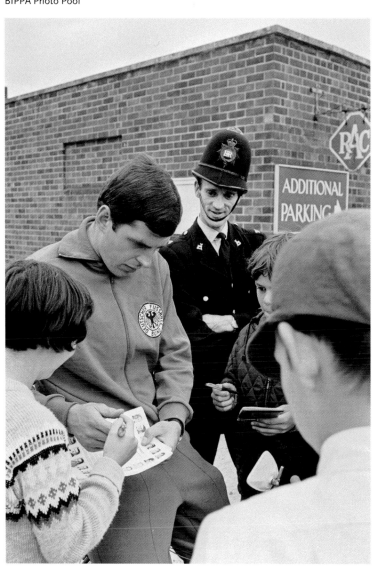

Thirteen minutes gone, 1-0 to West
Germany. Helmut Haller (centre of
trio) opens the scoring to the delight
of Franz Beckenbauer (to Haller's left)
and Wolfgang Overath. Consigned to
the stands the *Mirror* photographers
had to shoot around the arms and
heads of spectators
Monte Fresco/Kent Gavin, Mirror

Seventy-eight minutes gone, 2-1 to England. Martin Peters scores what looks like it could be a winning goal
Ron Bell, Press Association

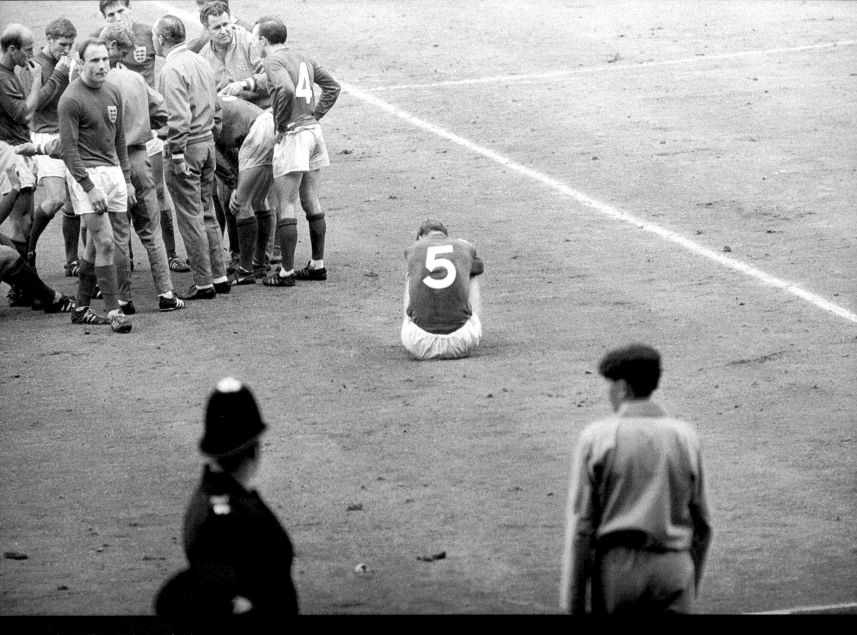

After Wolfgang Weber's 89th-minute equalizer, Alf Ramsey prepares for extra time and insists his players stand to show they are still strong – but a shattered Jack Charlton struggles to respond
Monte Fresco/Kent Gavin, Mirror

His troubles lifted, Jack Charlton skips
down the steps of the team coach to
the post-match reception at the Royal
Garden Hotel in Kensington
David Davies, Observer

**Martin Peters' shot leaves goalkeeper
Hans Tilkowski and Karl-Heinz
Schnellinger stranded for England's
second goal**

Gerry Cranham

**Bobby Charlton feels the pain of
120 minutes of hard graft**
Sven Simon

Descending the steps from the royal box, George Cohen is the player receiving a congratulatory hug and a pat on the head
Hans-Dietrich Kaiser, Nordbild

Franz Beckenbauer is consoled by manager Helmut Schön as defeat sinks in
Sven Simon

A crowd gathers outside the Royal Garden Hotel in Kensington in the hope of seeing the World Cup winners

Press Association

Muhammad Ali (as he has recently become, though he is still widely known as Cassius Clay) makes an appearance as the crowds stream along Wembley Way. In town to fight Brian London at Earls Court on 6 August, Ali doesn't appear to have stayed for the game
Mirror

One hundred minutes gone and
England's third goal, a shot from out
of the picture by Geoff Hurst, bounces
just behind the line, or possibly just
touching it depending on your point
of view. No picture or film footage is
100 per cent conclusive
Monte Fresco/Kent Gavin, Mirror

Geoff Hurst (left) claims the goal, backed up by Roger Hunt (centre). Willi Schulz leads the West German protests. The ball has bounced back in to play and no one yet knows the verdict – a goal, awarded by the so-called Russian linesman, Tofik Bakhramov from Azerbaijan

BIPPA Photo Pool

Previous page Confusion as photographers try to get a shot of the trophy aloft. Bobby Moore is obscured by Jack Charlton. The ubiquitous Wembley steward is on hand. The photographer on the right is Arthur Rickerby of Time Life

George Freston, Fox Photos

Wolfgang Weber looks back at
Wembley as the West Germans head
for the exit. On the left manager
Helmut Schön is consoling Sigi Held,
while Helmut Haller departs with the
matchball tucked under his arm.
German convention was that the first
goalscorer kept the ball. Thirty years
later, the *Mirror* newspaper mounted
such a vociferous campaign for its
return to Geoff Hurst that Haller had
little choice but to hand it over. A print
of this picture hangs in Weber's home
Hans Pfeil, Pfeil Foto

Bobby Moore takes a celebratory leap on the balcony of the Royal Garden Hotel
People

The England squad show off a replica
trophy from the balcony – the original
was under lock and key at a belatedly
security-conscious FA. This picture
made the front page of the *Sunday
Mirror* the following morning, 31 July

Mirror

The final whistle goes and the
England bench leap up. Manager
Alf Ramsey, however, stays seated as
reserve Jimmy Armfield attempts a
hug. On the far left Ramsey's West
German counterpart Helmut Schön
absorbs the scene while on the far
right Jimmy Greaves appears to have
mixed feelings
Gerry Cranham

Some people are on the pitch – the invaders who ran on in the last seconds of the game, prompting Kenneth Wolstenholme's famous BBC commentary. The cameras behind the goal are trained elsewhere, on Geoff Hurst, who is about to score England's fourth goal in the 119th and penultimate minute
Monte Fresco/Kent Gavin, Mirror

Among the fans, a cut-out World Cup Willie and a banner showing divided footballing loyalties

Gerry Cranham

The congratulations and
commiserations continue. Jimmy
Greaves and Alan Ball leaves the field
as Helmut Schön offers a handshake
Evening News

A broken-toothed admirer clings on to Bobby Moore as he passes the TV cameras
Neil Libbert, Sunday Times

**The morning after. Mr Geoff and Mrs
Judith Hurst pose for the cameras in
Kensington Gardens**

Terry Fincher, Express
©Getty Images

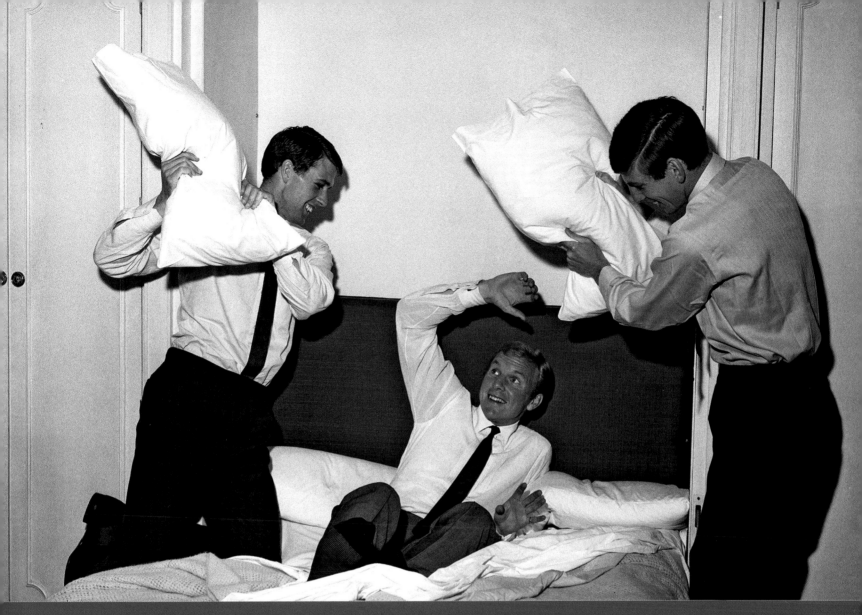

England's West Ham trio. Martin Peters (left) and Geoff Hurst batter Bobby Moore with pillows in the bedroom of the hotel the morning after the final. A knowing photographer sends-up a famous photograph of the Beatles taken by Harry Benson in 1964, when the band hit number one in the United States for the first time

Planet News

Alf Ramsey and wife Vicky talk over lunch the day after the final at an event in honour of England's victory staged by the ITV television team at the ATV Studios in Boreham Wood, Hertfordshire

Terry Fincher, Express
©Getty Images

Bobby Moore (left) and Bobby Charlton catch up with their wives, Tina and Norma respectively, at the Royal Garden Hotel celebrations. The wives had not been invited to the official dinner and dined separately

Reg Burkett, Express
©Getty Images

**The controversial third goal has been
given and Martin Peters lifts Geoff
Hurst in belated celebration while
Karl-Heinz Schnellinger is incredulous**
Evening Standard
©Getty Images

West Germany captain Uwe Seeler says goodbye to England – and to World Cup Willie – at the airport
George Stroud, Express
©Getty Images

Following page **The sun dips down over Wembley and the World Cup is drawing to an end**
Ray Green

1966
AFTERWORD

By Alan Bennett

Football hasn't always been the lifeblood of the nation and back in 1966 football in general and the World Cup in particular were quite easy to sidestep. The screen-watching crowds didn't spill out from pubs on to pavements and, at the great festivals of the Christian year, churches flew the flag of St George, but not taxi drivers or builders' merchants.

Still, in my parents' view far too much attention was paid to the game and to sport in general, particularly on television, which they had not all that long acquired. "Stinking sport," Dad would say, finding Kenneth Wolstenholme holding forth on some bleak provincial touchline. Mam felt the same, while later unwittingly registering football's increasing prominence in the life of the nation when she remarked (à propos of the extra-marital exploits of, I think, Tommy Docherty): "I see footballers are getting on with Other Women now."

In the light of which it's the more surprising that both my parents saw any of the 1966 World Cup final, let alone the crucial period of extra time. But Dad's dislike of sport admitted of one exception: TV wrestling. He had a regular appointment with the TV set late on Saturday afternoon when the likes of Massambula took on, say, Mick McManus or Jackie Pallo, with Massambula egged on by my father who, almost alone of the watching public, was convinced of the authenticity of the contest, the simple goodness of Massambula and the undiluted wickedness ("the bad sod") of McManus.

These contests were commentated upon by Kent Walton, an exotic and vaguely transatlantic figure, possibly Canadian but whom time has conflated in my mind with the singer Denis Lotis.

It was in the expectation of hearing Kent Walton and seeing his favourite villains that Dad had switched on the TV at the usual time only to find that "stinking football" was still going on (and on both channels) with extra time just starting. So when I arrived home later that evening, having listened to the match on the car radio en route from London, my parents were able to boast of what they had seen. "Your Mam and me got quite wound up," was how Dad described it. I was in time to watch with them as the team appeared on the balcony of the Royal Garden Hotel in Kensington, but I don't think we watched the re-run of the match.

As an initiation, the 1966 World Cup didn't take with my parents and I don't think they ever willingly watched football again, though until the end of his days Dad remained wrestling's most faithful fan.

Alan Bennett.

Dave Corbett – owner of Pickles –
settles down to watch the final with
his famous pet
John Downing, Express
©Getty Images

1966
RESULTS

NORTH EAST
Soviet Union 3 North Korea 0
Malofeyev 30 88, Banishevsky 31
12 July, Ayresome Park, 23,006

Italy 2 Chile 0
Mazzola 9, Barison 88
13 July, Roker Park, 27,199

Chile 1 North Korea 1
Marcos 27pen; Pak Seung-jin 88
15 July, Ayresome Park, 13,792

Soviet Union 1 Italy 0
Chislenko 57
16 July, Roker Park, 27,793

North Korea 1 Italy 0
Pak Doo-ik 41
19 July, Ayresome Park, 17,829

Soviet Union 2 Chile 1
Porkujan 29 87; Marcos 33
20 July, Roker Park, 16,027

Group D	P	W	D	L	F	A	Pts
Soviet Union	3	3	0	0	6	1	6
North Korea	3	1	1	1	2	4	3
Italy	3	1	0	2	2	2	2
Chile	3	0	1	2	2	5	1

Quarter-final
Soviet Union 2 Hungary 1
Chislenko 5, Porkujan 48; Bene 58
23 July, Roker Park, 22,103

The tournament odds are chalked up at the time of the draw on 6 January
Thomson Allied Newspapers,
Manchester

MIDLANDS
West Germany 5 Switzerland 0
Held 16, Haller 21 77pen,
Beckenbauer 40 62
12 July, Hillsborough, 36,127

Argentina 2 Spain 1
Artime 65 77; Roma 71og
13 July, Villa Park, 42,738

Spain 2 Switzerland 1
Sanchís 57, Amancio 75; Quentin 31
15 July, Hillsborough, 32,028

Argentina 0 West Germany 0
Sent off: Albrecht (Arg) 66
16 July, Villa Park, 46,587

Argentina 2 Switzerland 0
Artime 52, Onega 79
19 July, Hillsborough, 32,127

West Germany 2 Spain 1
Emmerich 39, Seeler 84; Fuste 23
20 July, Villa Park, 45,187

Group B	P	W	D	L	F	A	Pts
W Germany	3	2	1	0	7	1	5
Argentina	3	2	1	0	4	1	5
Spain	3	1	0	2	4	5	2
Switzerland	3	0	0	3	1	9	0

Quarter-final
West Germany 4 Uruguay 0
Haller 11 84, Beckenbauer 70, Seeler 77
Sent off: Troche (Uru) 50, Silva (Uru) 55
23 July, Hillsborough 40,007

NORTH WEST
Brazil 2 Bulgaria 0
Pelé 13, Garrincha 63
12 July, Goodison Park, 47,308

Portugal 3 Hungary 1
José Augusto 2 65, Torres 88; Bene 60
13 July, Old Trafford, 29,886

Hungary 3 Brazil 1
Bene 3, Farkas 64, Mészöly 72pen;
Tostão 15
15 July, Goodison Park, 51,387

Portugal 3 Bulgaria 0
Vutzov 7og, Eusébio 38, Torres 82
16 July, Old Trafford, 25,438

Portugal 3 Brazil 1
Simões 15, Eusébio 24 85; Rildo 71
19 July, Goodison Park, 58,479

Hungary 3 Bulgaria 1
Davidov 42og, Mészöly 44, Bene 53;
Asparoukhov 15
20 July, Old Trafford, 24,129

Group C	P	W	D	L	F	A	Pts
Portugal	3	3	0	0	9	2	6
Hungary	3	2	0	1	7	5	4
Brazil	3	1	0	2	4	6	2
Bulgaria	3	0	0	3	1	8	0

Quarter-final
Portugal 5 North Korea 3
Eusébio 26 43pen 57 60pen, José
Augusto 80; Pak Seung-jin 1, Lee
Dong-woon 20, Yang Sung-kook 24
23 July, Goodison Park, 40,248

Semi-final
West Germany 2 Soviet Union 1
Haller 43, Beckenbauer 68;
Porkujan 87
Sent off: Chislenko (Sov) 44
25 July, Goodison Park, 38,273

LONDON
England 0 Uruguay 0
11 July, Wembley, 87,148

France 1 Mexico 1
Hausser 61; Borja 48
13 July, Wembley, 69,237

Uruguay 2 France 1
Rocha 27, Cortés 32;
De Bourcoing 16pen
15 July, White City, 45,662

England 2 Mexico 0
R Charlton 36, Hunt 76
16 July, Wembley 92,570

Mexico 0 Uruguay 0
19 July, Wembley, 61,112

England 2 France 0
Hunt 36 76
20 July, Wembley, 98,270

Group A	P	W	D	L	F	A	Pts
England	3	2	1	0	4	0	5
Uruguay	3	1	2	0	2	1	4
Mexico	3	0	2	1	1	3	2
France	3	0	1	2	2	5	1

Quarter-final
England 1 Argentina 0
Hurst 77
Sent off: Rattín (Arg) 36
23 July, Wembley, 90,584

Semi-final
England 2 Portugal 1
R Charlton 30 79; Eusébio 82pen
26 July, Wembley, 94,493

Third-place final
Portugal 2 Soviet Union 1
Eusébio 13pen, Torres 88; Malofeyev 44
28 July, Wembley, 87,696

Final
England 4 West Germany 2
Hurst 19 100 119, Peters 78;
Haller 13, Weber 89
30 July, Wembley, 93,802, after extra time

1966
PHOTOGRAPHY

The how and who of covering the World Cup
Compiled by Peter Robinson

THE BASICS

Access to games for photographers was restricted by the decision of the organizing committee (on the advice of the FA) to limit their number at each game to 23 at Wembley (27 for the final) and 18 elsewhere. This led to a pool system, with the newspapers and others sharing their production. In addition, in the 40 years since the tournament, many photo agencies and newspapers have changed hands or merged. Records have been lost and archives disposed of, sometimes separately to the papers that originally commissioned the work.

As a result it has been impossible to confirm the precise origin of some images; there are some joint credits, where people worked together.

There were set numbers of passes for overseas photographers, then four separate UK pools: BIPPA, the British International Photographic Press Agencies; the Newspaper Proprietors' Association (NPA) for the national press; the Newspaper Society for regional papers; and the Periodical Publishers' Association (PPA) for magazines. Each group appointed one party to distribute the images chosen for publication. To complicate matters further, pool photos were passed to another pool if requested. This has resulted in many images, notably from the final, being in the possession of numerous agencies and papers, with the exact origin unknown. Allocations were as follows.

All venues except Wembley: 18 photographers
From the countries playing – four each; NPA – two; Newspaper Soc – two; PPA – two; BIPPA – four.

England's Wembley games: 23 photographers
Opponents' country – eight; NPA – four; Newspaper Soc – four; PPA – three; BIPPA – four.

Other Wembley games: 23 photographers
Competing countries – five each; NPA – three; Newspaper Soc – three; PPA – three; BIPPA – four.

The final: 27 photographers
With one or two exceptions, we have established the identities of all the accredited photographers. West Germany – 12. Otto Mettelmann (*Kicker*), Ludwig Gayer, Ferdi Hartung, Horst Müller, Sven Simon, Hans Dietrich Kaiser (Nordbild), Norbert Seiffert (Schirner), Werner Rhehacek (Werek), Erich Baumann, Dieter Frinke, Willi Gutberlet (DPA), Heinz Pfeil (Pfeilfoto).

NPA – four. Neil Libbert (*Sunday Times*) and Norman Quicke (*Sunday Express*) plus, it is thought, Arthur Jones (*Evening Standard*) and Dennis Hart (*Evening News*).
Newspaper Soc – four. Tony Harris, Mark Seymour, Ron Bell (all PA) plus one unknown, though Derek Cattani was present as FA official photographer.
PPA – three. Arthur Rickerby (*Life* magazine, USA) Gerry Cranham (*Illustrated London News*), George Freston (Fox).
BIPPA – four. Lol Harris, Les Priest (both AP), Herbie Ludford, Didier Bragard (both UPI).
It should be noted that others shot from the stands and anecdotes survive of various improvised techniques to gain access.

THE AGENCIES
BIPPA

Managed the agency pool, handling material from the major press agencies: Keystone Press, Central Press, Associated Press, United Press International and Sport & General. They hired four photographers per region – one for each corner of the ground.
North East Ted West (Central), Maurice Sayers (UPI), Eddie Raymond (Keystone), Raul Fornetsa (AP Rome).
North West Garry Weaser, Doug Miller (both Keystone), Charlie Dawson (UPI), Bob Rider (AP).
Midlands Brian Calvert (AP), Brian Thomas, Vic Fowler (both S&G), Gerhard Seinig (UPI Frankfurt).
London Lol Harris, Les Priest (both AP), Herbie Ludford (UPI), Didier Bragard (UPI Brussels).
BIPPA's 1966 World Cup material remains substantially intact in the Hulton Archive, which was acquired by Getty Images in 1996.

KEYSTONE PRESS AGENCY

Founded in 1920 by "Bert" Garai, a Hungarian, Keystone Press was the UK's first international picture agency. Home of many of the defining images of 20th century press photography. Acquired by the Hulton Archive in 1988. Along with Eddie Raymond, their 1966 photographers included:
Garry Weaser Born in 1940, he started in the PA darkroom then worked for the *Ilford Recorder* before joining Keystone in 1965. Left after 15 years for the *Guardian*, where he worked till 2002.

Doug Miller Born in 1905 and a star Keystone man. British Press Photographer of the Year in 1954. Won a World Press Award in 1969 for his picture of Bob Beamon breaking the long jump record at the 1968 Olympic Games in Mexico City. Died in 1977.
Jimmy Gray A dispatch rider, darkroom man, wire operator (transmitting pictures) then finally a photographer for Keystone. Later had 25 years at the *Daily Mail*, 12 as their royal photographer.

CENTRAL PRESS PHOTOS

Established in 1914 as a news photo agency by Percy Hay, former picture editor of the *Daily Mirror*. Became a sub-agency of Keystone Press in 1976, operating until 1982. Known 1966 photographer:
Ted West Born in London in 1933, he started at the *Evening Standard* as a messenger and was later a darkroom assistant. Joined Central Press in 1962 and had 27 years at the *Guardian* from 1970.

FOX PHOTOS

Established in 1926 as a general press agency. The PPA, the only pool that had an outlet for colour photography (all papers were black and white), selected Fox to act for them at the final. Became part of Keystone in 1984. Their 1966 men included:
George Freston Born in 1934, Freston joined Fox in 1949. He and some colleagues purchased the company in 1972. It is believed that the famous image in colour of Bobby Moore and the team with the cup may be his work. Freston died in 2004.

SPORT & GENERAL

Believed to the world's oldest specialist sports photography agency. Established in 1895 and active until 1996. S&G was the only photo agency allowed access to Lord's cricket ground from the 1930s up to 1972. Distributed by Empics (now part of PA) since 2001. Their 1966 men included:
Brian Thomas Born 1933 in Windsor, went from school to the S&G mail room as a runner. Returned after national service as a printer, becoming a full-time photographer in 1956. Joined the *News of the World* in 1968, staying there until retirement in1995. His best remembered football picture was of a dog relieving itself against the goal post during a West Ham v Liverpool game in the 1970s.

Photographers pursue Bobby Moore around Wembley. In the foreground AP man Lol Harris wrestles with his cameras
Derek Cattani,
Fox Photos

Vic Fowler Joined S&G at 14 in 1946 as a messenger. After a period as a darkroom printer and national service, became a photographer in 1953. With S&G for 20 years, then moved to the *Sunday Independent* in Plymouth, working with a young reporter named Alastair Campbell. He continued to freelance into his late sixties.

ASSOCIATED PRESS
The US equivalent of the Press Association, who also operate internationally. Their 1966 men were Bob Dear, Bob Rider, Raul Fornetsa (Rome bureau), Brian Calvert, Lol Harris and Les Priest. Now distributed by PA through Empics.

UNITED PRESS INTERNATIONAL
Major American news agency which incorporated Planet News. Their 1966 men were Peter Skingley, Maurice Sayers, Charlie Dawson, Gerhard Seinig (Frankfurt), Herbie Ludford and Didier Bragard (Belgium). Closed 1970, archive now with Topfoto.

PRESS ASSOCIATION
Founded in 1868, the PA provide news and photographs to their many subscribers, including all the national press. As one of the largest media organizations, the PA had many photographers covering the World Cup through the Newspaper Society pool and their material is now distributed by Empics. Their 1966 photographers were:
Denis Evans Born in 1925, Evans's first job was as a messenger at Associated Press, by whom he was hired during World War II on the recommendation of Len Puttnam (the father of David, now Lord, Puttnam), then an AP war photographer. Evans was initially paid 28 shillings (£1.40) a week. He joined the PA in 1956 and retired in 1988. His most celebrated picture was of Roger Bannister running the sub-four-minute mile at Oxford in 1954.
Reg Bagnall PA staff photographer in Yorkshire, who worked with Evans in Sheffield in 1966 and received an MBE in 1989.
Eric Shaw Born in 1928 in Salford. From school became a runner for the *Manchester Evening Chronicle*. After national service, a printer at the *Chronicle*. Worked for the PA from 1954 to 1990, receiving an MBE for services to journalism in 1990.

Ron Bell Joined Fox Photos at 15 in 1946 as a photographic printer. After national service in the RAF photo section, rejoined Fox as a photographer. After a spell at UPI, worked for the PA till he retired. British Press Photographer of the Year in 1975, the year he became the PA's royal photographer. Was awarded the Royal Victorian Order. Died in 2001.
George Stephenson Joined Topical Press Agency in the darkroom at 16 in 1931. A photographer in the Army map-making unit in the Middle East in World War II. In 1946 joined PA Reuters as a photographer and worked there until retirement. Former British Press Photographer of the Year. Died in 1981.
Tony Harris Starting as a PA messenger aged 15 in 1951, became a darkroom printer then, in 1964, a staff photographer. Later freelanced for the PA and the *Daily Express*.
Johnny Horton Also worked for the PA on the 1966 World Cup. His famous 1956 picture of Tom Finney casting a shower of spray as he played was the basis for a statue unveiled at Preston in 2002.
Derek Millward, Mark Seymour, Wally Lockyear, Nick Beer London-based PA men whose photography is featured in this book.

POPPERFOTO
Founded in 1934 by Paul Popper, Popperfoto was operating as a news agency in 1966 and represented Planet News. However, the majority of the pictures in this book are subsequent acquisitions. Now termed popperfoto.com, it was purchased in 1990 by sports photographer Bob Thomas. Popperfoto still own half of the Planet News archive, as well as material credited in the book to Pedro De Lima – a Brazilian photographic agent – and Ray Green.
Ray Green Born in Sheffield, 1928, graduated through local press to the *Observer* and later the *Sunday Times* colour magazine, but remained freelance and based in the north. Not exclusively a sports man, but one of the first to specialise in creative football photography. Got a ticket for the final and shot from the stands. He died in 1985.

SYNDICATION INTERNATIONAL
Part of the Mirror group, sold *Mirror* photographs and bespoke commissioned photography to third parties. Now part of the *Mirror* archive, Mirrorpix.

NATIONAL NEWSPAPERS
DAILY & SUNDAY MIRROR
At the time, owned by the International Publishing Corporation, whose name survives as the publisher IPC. The *Mirror* papers have changed hands several times, but the photographic archive remains with the titles. Along with Ernie Chapman and Charlie Ley, *Mirror* men whose work is featured are:
Monte Fresco Born in London in 1936, from school Fresco became a runner for the photo agency Topical Press. He joined the *Daily Mirror* in 1957, retiring as chief sports photographer in 1988. Shot the 1966 final from the stands, with Kent Gavin. In 2003 he was given a lifetime achievement award for services to sports photography and has an MBE.
Eric Piper Took some of the most famous news photographs of the 1970s when he travelled to Cambodia with the journalist John Pilger and documented the crimes of the Khmer Rouge. "A photographer who never, to my knowledge, owned a camera bag, preferring plastic airline bags," his famous colleague has said. Piper died in 1982.
John Varley Born in 1934 in Doncaster, Varley joined the *Yorkshire Evening News* at 14, then worked for the *Daily Mirror* in Yorkshire from 1959 until his retirement in 1988. Covered many World Cups and numerous news assignments, including the 1967-70 Biafran war. Managed to photograph the final, by his own devices, shooting in colour.
Peter Sheppard Born in 1930 in Nottingham, Sheppard worked on newspapers in Mansfield, King's Lynn and Newcastle. Later worked for the *Daily Mirror* for 21 years. Still freelancing in 2005.
Charles Owens Joined the *Mirror* aged 21 in 1957 and stayed with the paper until retirement.
Tom Buist His first published photograph was in 1949, aged 11, in the *Edinburgh Evening News*. Joined the Scottish *Daily Express* darkroom three years later, the *Glasgow Herald* in 1958, the *Daily Sketch* in 1961 and the Manchester office of the *Daily Mirror* in 1964. Has been freelancing in Northumberland since leaving the *Mirror* in 1988.
Kent Gavin Born in 1939. Started at Keystone as a messenger, where he worked as a photographer after national service. With the *Mirror* from 1965 to 2004. British Press Photographer of the Year four times, Royal Photographer of the Year seven times.

DAILY & SUNDAY EXPRESS

One of the most prolific picture desks in Fleet Street at the time, with more than 60 photographers. The *Express* archives were acquired by Hulton in 1983 and 1990. Their 1966 men included:

Terry Fincher Joined Keystone as a messenger in 1945 then became a staff photographer. Moved to the *Daily Herald* in 1958 then the *Daily Express* in 1962. He left the *Express* in 1969 to form his own company, Photographers International. Was named British Press Photographer of the Year four times.

John Downing Born in 1940 in Llanelli. British Press Photographer of the Year seven times and awarded an MBE in 1992 for services to journalism. Left the *Daily Express* in 2001 as chief photographer after over 20 years on the staff. Currently freelance.

Clive Limpkin Born in 1937 in Croydon, he had a brief career in forestry then entered journalism via a sports literary agency. He worked for the *Eagle* comic, the *Daily Express*, *Daily Sketch* and the *Sun*, before becoming a *Daily Mail* staff photographer. Was also a feature writer on the *Sunday Times* and the *Observer*. His photographic book *The Battle of Bogside*, showing the fighting in Northern Ireland, won the Robert Capa Gold Medal for 1972; his photograph of the first topless girl in the *Sun* has yet to receive any official recognition.

Bob Stiggins, Norman Quicke Staff sports photographers, who both shot the 1966 final.

George Stroud The staff photographer based at London airport, now known as Heathrow, covering the arrivals and departures of the famous.

Ron Viner Birmingham-based staff photographer.

Reg Burkett A staff photographer, much of whose work was for the *Sunday Express*.

THE GUARDIAN

Two years before the World Cup, the paper moved its headquarters from Manchester to London. It has been owned by the Scott Trust, rather than a limited company, since 1936.

THE OBSERVER

Owned at the time by the Astor family, the Sunday title is now part of the Guardian Media Group and its photographic archive from 1966 has become contained within that of its daily sister title.

TIMES & SUNDAY TIMES

Owned by Lord Thomson in 1966, sold to Rupert Murdoch in 1981, with picture archives intact.

Neil Libbert Born in 1938 and educated at Manchester School of Art. After freelancing, took a staff position on what was then the *Manchester Guardian* in 1958, leaving in 1965. He freelanced for the *Sunday Times* for many years and now works for the *Observer*. Covered the final.

THE SUN

In 1964 the broadsheet *Daily Herald*, which had been bought by the Mirror Group, was closed and relaunched as the *Sun*. In 1969 Rupert Murdoch bought the title, but not the photo archive, which is now part of Mirrorpix. 1966 photographers:

George Phillips The son of the *New York Times* photographer Cecil Phillips, George joined the Planet News agency in 1950 aged 16 and shot the funeral of King George VI two years later. After a spell at the *People*, joined the *Sun* in 1965. Later freelanced for *Today*, the *Sun* and the *Daily Mirror*.

Peter Ralph A staff photographer in Liverpool.

THE PEOPLE

Its archive belongs to the Mirror group, the paper's current publishers.

REGIONAL NEWSPAPERS

EVENING STANDARD

Owned in 1966, like the *Express* titles, by the Beaverbrook family. The *Standard*'s archives were purchased by Hulton in 1983 and 1985; the title was bought by Associated Newspapers in 1980.

EVENING NEWS

This London paper, long owned by the publishers of the *Daily Mail*, was closed in 1980 after its proprietors bought its rival, the *Evening Standard*. The photographic archive has been dispersed.

SUNDERLAND ECHO

Gerry Rennison Born in 1909, the long-standing chief photographer on the paper retired in 1974 and died in 1980.

Eddie Pears Born in 1915, Pears succeeded Rennison as chief photographer. He died in 1993.

Tony Colling Joined the *Echo* aged 15 in 1959 and still working for the paper in 2005.

John Forbes Aged 42 in 1966, covering Durham.

BIRMINGHAM POST & MAIL

Gerry Armes Born in 1928, worked for 40 years mainly as a sports photographer on the staff of Birmingham newspapers. Followed the Argentina squad extensively in 1966, a role that involved acting as Alfredo Di Stefano's unofficial chauffeur.

Jeff Heath Chief photographer on the *Post*.

LIVERPOOL POST & ECHO

Stephen Shakeshaft On the staff since arriving as a 16-year-old in 1962. Won the Royal Picture of the Year award, currently picture editor of both papers.

OTHER REGIONAL SOURCES

The *Northern Echo*, a Darlington-based paper; Mercury Press, a Liverpool-based news agency; and Thomson Regional Newspapers.

OVERSEAS SOURCES
NORDBILD

Hans-Dietrich Kaiser Born in 1927, he started with the agency Schirner then formed his own business, Nordbild, in 1957. He covered all the World Cups from 1958 to 1974. He was a prizewinner at the 1966 World Press Awards. Nordbild was bought by the Witters agency, with UK distribution by Offside.

PHOTOPRESS ARCHIV A Swiss company set up in the 1930s that was acquired by Keystone Zurich in 1980 (a different company to Keystone UK).

L'EQUIPE France's sports daily, the country's second largest-selling paper. UK distribution by Offside. Their 1966 men were:

Andre Lecoq Worked in the *L'Equipe* laboratory until 1960 and then became a staff photographer. He stayed with the paper until 1996, when he was 61.

Robert Legros Was with *L'Equipe* from the late Fifties until 1994, when he was 65.

A BOLA Portugal's most popular sports daily, with a readership of more than 800,000. Their work is distributed through ASF. Their 1966 man was:

Nuno Ferrari (Nuno José da Fonseca Ferreira)
Took his name from Amadeu Ferrari, a former
celebrated sports photographer. Starting his career
in 1953, aged 18, he covered the 1966, 1982 and
1986 World Cups. He died in 1996, suffering a heart
attack while covering Benfica v Porto at the Stadium
of Light. A Lisbon street is named after him.

OTHER FOREIGN SOURCES
Farabolafoto, a Milan-based Italian agency, with UK
distribution by Offside and DPA, the German Press
Association.

INDIVIDUAL PHOTOGRAPHERS

SVEN SIMON Born 1941, the son of the German
newspaper publisher Axel Springer. He worked as a
photographer and picture agent under his
pseudonym and later edited the newspaper *Welt
am Sonntag*, before committing suicide in 1980.

GERRY CRANHAM Born in 1929. Twice Sports
Photographer of the Year and a fellow of the Royal
Photographic Society. His work is in the permanent
collection of the Victoria & Albert Museum.

HEINZ PFIEL Born in 1922, this German freelance
sports photographer, now retired, set up his own
agency, Pfiel Foto. He shot eight World Cups from
1954 to 1982. His picture on pages 228-9 has pride
of place on Wolfgang Weber's sitting-room wall.

NEIL LEIFER Born in New York in 1942, perhaps
the most famous sports photographer in the world.
Despite working for *Sports Illustrated*, he had to
cover the 1966 final from the stands. However, his
image of the Muhammad Ali v Cleveland Williams
fight taken four months later, shot by remote
control from overhead with Williams knocked out,
is seen as the greatest sports photograph ever.

DEREK CATTANI He was on the staff of the
Football Association as their official photographer
in 1966. His office at the FA was next door to that of
Alf Ramsey, for whom he made numerous cups of
tea. Most of his exclusive pictures covering the
period before and after the World Cup triumph
were destroyed by a fire in 1970.

PHOTOGRAPHY CREDITS

*Original photographers and sources appear beneath the respective photographs where known.
The copyright holders/distributors are listed below. Page number followed by 'a' 'b' = 'top' 'bottom' or
'left' 'right'. page number followed by 'a' 'b' 'c' 'd' = clockwise from top left*

Getty Images *www.gettyimages.com/archival*
Photos bylined BIPPA, Keystone, Fox Photos,
Express, Evening Standard
Front & back cover, p22-3, 26b, 28a, 28b, 30c, 30d,
31, 35, 36-7, 40, 41a, 41b, 41c, 41d, 46, 47, 50, 51,
55, 59, 63, 66, 67, 71b, 76a, 76b, 77, 80b, 80-1, 85,
86a, 86b, 86c, 86d, 87, 90a, 93, 95a, 95b, 95c, 95d,
97, 99, 100, 108, 112, 114-5, 116, 118-9, 123a, 123b,
126, 127, 129, 132-3, 133, 134, 135, 137, 138a,
138b, 144c, 144d, 146b, 147, 152, 153, 155, 159,
162, 163, 166, 178, 182-3, 184, 185, 187, 189b,
192-3, 194-5, 199, 200-1, 203, 207, 209, 211, 212a,
224-5, 227, 238, 240a, 240b, 241, 242, 243, 246, 251

Empics *www.empics.com*
Photos bylined Press Association, Associated Press
p19, 24a, 29, 34a, 34b, 43, 58, 60-1, 72-3, 74, 78, 83,
94, 96-7, 102, 103, 109, 118, 120a, 121, 122-3, 130-1,
144a, 144b, 148-9, 154, 164, 172, 177, 181, 182,
186, 188, 189a, 190, 191, 196, 197, 212b, 215, 222

Mirrorpix *www.mirrorpix.com*
Photos bylined Mirror, Sun, Syndication
International, People
p2, 23, 26-7, 36, 44, 45, 48-9, 54, 88-9, 106-7, 110,
111, 120b, 128, 136, 145, 150, 150-1, 156-7, 160,
168-9, 171, 173, 176, 192, 198, 204-5, 206, 214, 216,
223, 226, 230, 230-1, 234

Offside *www.welloffside.com*
Photos bylined Farabolafoto, Nordbild, L'Equipe
p14, 15, 42, 71a, 98a, 98b, 101, 117, 125, 138-9,
161, 170, 174, 180, 210, 220

Popperfoto *www.popperfoto.com*
Photos bylined Planet News, Ray Green,
Pedro De Lima
p12, 140-1, 165, 167, 175, 239, 244-5

Keystone (Switzerland) *www.keystone.ch*
Photos bylined Photopress Archiv
p64, 65, 69, 79, 84, 90b

Sunderland Echo p16, 17, 18, 20-1, 24b, 25, 26a,
30a, 30b, 32-3, 39, 52, 53, 56-7, 57,

Birmingham Post & Mail p62, 68a ,68b, 75a, 75b,
80a, 82, 91, 92, 104, 104-5,

Gerry Cranham p202, 218-9, 232-3, 235, 256
ASF (Portugal) p113, 143, 146a
The Guardian Spine, p158, 217
Imago *www.imago-stock.de* p219, 221
Peter Robinson p6,11
Science & Society Picture Library
www.scienceandsociety.co.uk p13, 124
Topfoto *www.topfoto.co.uk* p5,179
Ullstein *www.ullsteinbild.de* p9, 208
DPA *www.dpa.com* p70
Neil Leifer p213
Liverpool Post & Echo p142
NI Syndication/Neil Libbert p237
Northern Echo p38
Hans Pfeil p228-9
Solo Syndication p236
Thomson Allied Newspapers p248

*All reasonable attempt has been made to ensure the information is
correct. If there are any errors please contact the publishers*

1966 INDEX

ACKNOWLEDGEMENTS

In addition to those listed in the photography section, the authors would like to thank the many photographers who worked on the 1966 World Cup but due to lack of space or dispersal of their work we were unable to include: Ron Ashurst, Gordon Amory, Peter Arnold, Chris Barham, Ron Burton, Peter Cook, Albert Cooper, Guus De Jong, Leo Dillon, Peter Dunne, Larry Ellis, Barry Farrell, Norman Finnegan, Kevin Fitzpatrick, Ron Fortune, Barry Henson, Ron Hope, David Jameson, James Larkin, Aubrey Matthews, Bill Mealey, Terry Mealey, Billy Payne, Neville Pyne, Arthur Rickerby, Brian Robinson, John Robson, Lorenzo Rodriguez (who shot every World Cup 1930 – 1966), Ron Sanders, Chris Smith, Colin Theakston, Geoff Thomas, Wilf Thompson, Tony Triolo, Charlie Westburg

Special thanks to all the following for their help bringing *1966 Uncovered* to publication: Alex Anderfuhren, Jon Asbury, Paul Atkinson, Mel Attrill, Bob Aylott, Roger Bamber, Frank Baron, Franz Beckenbauer, Alan Bennett, Ian Berry, Ian Blackwell, Anna Burke, Matthew Butson, Bryn Campbell, Sarah Carver, Dave Caulkin, Terry Chambers, Don Chapman, Bobby Charlton, Keith Cooper, Philip Cornwall, Peter Crookston, Ulrich Cruwell, Ian Curry, Jaap de Groot, Johnny Eggitt, Adam Ganz, Julian Germaine, Simon Gill, Alan Glenwright, Annabel Gordon, Lucy Gosling, Tim Graham, Leslie Graves, Betty Green, Edd Griffin, Richard Guy, Thomas Hackbarth, Tony Hall, Peter Hannan, Martin Harrison, Ulrich Hesse-Lichtenberger, David Hurn, Simon Inglis, Ruth Kitchin, John Knill, Reg Lancaster, Les Lee, Mark Leech, Howie Leifer, David Levenson, Norman Luck, Marianne Maini, Tony Mancini, Ems Magnus, Nigel Matheson, Chris Morphet, Phil O'Brien, Trevor Owens, Norman Potter, David Puttnam, Randolf Pfeil, Frank Plowright, Paul Rennie, Hilda Richards, Wanda Rickerby, Per Rumberg, Kevin Royal, Jane Salt, Tony Sapiano, Ken Saunders, Phil Sheldon, Neal Simpson, Neville Smith, Marina Spickermann, Stanneylands Hotel, Susan Swinney, Rob Taggart, Jack Taylor, Alan Thorpe, Denis Thorpe, Alex Timms, Phil Town, Tom Tyrell, Mike Wells, Geoffrey White, Valeria Witters, Gary Woodhouse, Arthur Wooster, Geoff Wright

Alf Ramsey takes the Jules Rimet trophy down the Wembley tunnel
Gerry Cranham